Living Deep
in a
Shallow World

Sanford Zensen

WIPF & STOCK · Eugene, Oregon

LIVING DEEP IN A SHALLOW WORLD

Copyright © 2020 Sanford Zensen. All rights reserved. Except for brief quotations in critical publications or reviews, no part of this book may be reproduced in any manner without prior written permission from the publisher. Write: Permissions, Wipf and Stock Publishers, 199 W. 8th Ave., Suite 3, Eugene, OR 97401.

Wipf & Stock
An Imprint of Wipf and Stock Publishers
199 W. 8th Ave., Suite 3
Eugene, OR 97401

www.wipfandstock.com

PAPERBACK ISBN: 978-1-7252-8938-3
HARDCOVER ISBN: 978-1-7252-8939-0
EBOOK ISBN: 978-1-7252-8940-6

Manufactured in the U.S.A.

Dedication

For my two wonderful granddaughters, Madison and Courtney, the joys of my heart—a heart that desires above all else that you become deep women of faith who will *"love the Lord your God with all your heart, all your soul, all your mind, and all your strength"* and love people as God loves you (cf. Matt. 22:37-40, NLT). The whole of life is wrapped up in these two commandments.

Walk with the King.

"Now to him who is able to keep you from stumbling and to present you blameless before the presence of his glory with great joy, to the only God, our Savior, through Jesus Christ our Lord, be glory, majesty, dominion, and authority, before all time and now and forever. Amen" (Jude 24-25, ESV).

"May the Lord bless you and protect you.
May the Lord smile on you and be gracious to you.
May the Lord show you his favor and give you his peace"
(Num. 6:24-26, NLT).

About the Author

Sanford "Sandy" Zensen is an ordained Baptist and former Christian & Missionary Alliance minister with 20+ years' experience in pastoral ministry. In addition, he has served 25 years as a professor of Christian studies and a Christian college administrator, continuing to teach as an adjunct professor for two separate institutions. He holds two professional degrees, MDiv (Gordon-Conwell Theological Seminary) and DMin (Luther Rice Seminary) and a PhD in religion and society (Oxford/Omega Graduate School).

Sandy is a frequent speaker at churches, men's events, and college alumni functions. He was the 2014 AGS (Adult and Graduate Studies) commencement speaker at Bryan College (Tennessee). In December 2019, Sandy's first book, *On the Wall with Sword and Trowel* (WIPF and Stock) was released and has received five-star reviews. He continues to serve as a member and Sunday school teacher at Stuart Heights Baptist Church, one of the largest Southern Baptist churches in the Chattanooga, Tennessee, area.

Table of Contents

Introduction 9

Chapter 1
    Personal Assessment—How Deep Am I?. 17

Chapter 2
    Eternity on My Eyeballs 27

Chapter 3
    What Really Counts. 39

Chapter 4
    Let My Heart Be Broken 49

Chapter 5
    Settle Down 59

Chapter 6
    Let It Go—Forgiveness 71

Chapter 7
    When Common Isn't Good Enough. 83

Chapter 8
    A Light Unto My Path. 95

Chapter 9
    Talking Things Over with God 111

Chapter 10
    A Living and Holy Sacrifice 133

Chapter 11
    Turn the World Right Side Up! 143

Chapter 12
    Sounding the Alarm 157

Epilogue 169

> *"It's not great talents nor great learning nor great preachers that God needs—men great in holiness, great in faith, great in love, great in fidelity, great for God…The Church is looking for better methods; God is looking for better men."*[1]
>
> – E. M. Bounds

Introduction

In his classic, *Celebration of Discipline*, Richard J. Foster wrote the following:

Superficiality is the curse of our age. The doctrine of instant satisfaction is a primary spiritual problem. The desperate need today is not for a greater number of intelligent people. Or gifted people. But for deep people.[2]

When I first read that remark I thought, *Lord, I want to be one of those! A deep person. A disciplined man. I want my last few years to count for something more than they have in the past.* I readily admit my life has not been what it should have been or could have been. It's that simple. I confess to spiritual ineptness and certainly shallowness—at times, *"half-hearted and wavering"* in my faith (James 1:8, TPT). Superficiality seems to follow me everywhere. In the parable of the sower and the soil, Jesus spoke of people with *"no depth of soil,"* who *"withered away"* when the heat of the day was turned up. They did not survive for long because *"they had no root"* (Matt. 13:5-6, ESV). That assessment hits just a bit too close to home.

John Eldredge noted,

> There is a secret set within each of our hearts…It is the desire for life as it was meant to be…a yearning for things to be right…something in us longs, hopes, maybe even at times believes that this is not the way things were supposed to be. Our desire fights the assault of death upon life…At some deep level, we refuse to accept the fact that this is the way things are, or must be, or always will be.[3]

I agree. Life is not what it's "supposed to be." Consequently, I want something more, something better, something deeper. Things can change. Life can change. I can change…under the empowering and direction of the Word and Spirit of God. In truth, I need to go deeper with Him.

"Deep people" live life as God intended—identifying and embracing significant, meaningful pursuits and biblical objectives in their personal and professional lives, spending their days wisely, avoiding damnable impulses, trivial concerns, and shallow thinking, and applying the gospel accurately and effectively across current cultural issues and problems. I want to be that kind of man—a deep person who loves the broken-hearted with compassion in my heart and a cup of cold water in my hand. I want to feel deeply with those who are hurting and suffering, to be quick to mercifully administer the healing *"balm of Gilead"* (Jer. 8:22) to a wounded heart. I want to be useful in making the peace of God real in an uncertain world and to demonstrate in word and deed just how deep and wide the love and mercy of God is. I want to smarten-up more and engage the human intellect with the

Introduction

truth and trustworthiness of the Scriptures. I want it all—everything a deep person is capable of being. I want to reach beyond the ordinary, to the way life was meant to be—the self-life crucified, dead and gone and the Christ-life, alive and functioning well.

David W. McCullough *(The Trivialization of God)* warned, "Our obsession with self has led us astray into the temple of idols: in particular, (the) god-of-my-comfort, god-of-my-success, the god who can help me get what I want." These are the gods of shallow thinkers. McCullough then quoted Princeton sociologist Robert Wuthnow, who put shallow living in perspective.

> At one time theologians argued that the chief purpose of humankind was to glorify God. Now it would seem that the logic has been reversed: the chief purpose of God is to glorify humankind. Spirituality no longer is true or good because it meets absolute standards of truth or goodness, but because it helps me get along. I am the judge of its worth. If it helps me find a vacant parking space, I know my spirituality is on the right track. If it leads me into the wilderness, calling me to face dangers I would rather not deal with at all, then it is a form of spirituality I am unlikely to choose.[4]

Superficiality is all too common in every age and culture. Nonetheless, from its inception Christianity has remained defiantly a bit too costly, too intrusive, too demanding for many who would rather have *"the appearance of godliness, but* [deny] *its power"* (II Tim 3:5, ESV). Shallowness devalues human worth, discounts men and women as image-bearers of God, ignores the personal dignity of every human being, and downplays the significant role each one plays in the world. We need to be deeper people. We must do better. I must be better. "We need men (and women) of the cross, with the message of the cross, bearing the marks of the cross."[5]

Os Guinness observed in his book *The Call*, "The trouble is that as modern people, we have too much to live with and too little to live for."[6] How insightful and painfully true. This truth became evident to me at a summer softball tournament for seven- to eight-year-old girls. If you ever want to see the depravity of man for what it is—stripped of pretense—get to one of these events and observe the parents in the stands and the coaches in the dugouts. It can be an ugly, disappointing sight.

I was making my way to the concession stand between games when I noticed a coach gathering his team of little girls around him—all wide-eyed, waiting for him to say something profound that might motivate them to play harder and win the next game. The coach brought the girls in close. I was intrigued, so I stuck around on the fringe of the team huddle to listen. He said, "Now repeat after me—everybody together, '1-2-3 TROPHIES!'" The girls yelled on cue as instructed. Enthusiastic, but clueless.

I thought, *That's it? That's all you got?? Nothing else? That's what they're playing for?* How trivial. How unimportant. How shallow.

Don't get me wrong. I'm as competitive as the next guy, but I remember John Stonestreet, now president of the Colson Center for Christian Worldview, speaking as a young man to his college graduating class. He suggested a much different approach to life's values and pursuits. He quoted his high school baseball coach to make his point: "I am not afraid of failure. I am afraid of succeeding at something that doesn't matter." Well, me too. I want something more out of life than a few passing moments of glory and some tarnished trophies. Frankly, who cares in the long run.

Introduction

William Wallace, the Scottish revolutionary, refused to submit to English rule. He would not under any circumstance compromise his convictions and the principles upon which he had built his life and leadership. Eventually, he was captured by English troops and condemned to die for high treason. Near the conclusion of the movie *Braveheart*, Wallace was chained to a dungeon wall, awaiting his execution. He was to be beheaded the next morning but not before the pain and humiliation of public torture (including being hung upside down, emasculated, eviscerated, drawn and quartered and his bowels burned before him.)[7]

He was visited by King Edward's daughter-in-law, Princess Isabella, who came to the prison to plead with Wallace to reconsider his position. Maybe the king would be merciful and order a quick execution, she suggested—if Wallace would simply capitulate to the king's demands and recognize his rulership and authority over Scotland. "Who knows what can happen," she said, "if you can only live." His response was powerful and revealed a character of extraordinary depth.

He replied, "If I swear to him, then all that I am is dead already." The man would not bend to tyranny. He would not budge under threat of execution. He would not surrender his ideals. He was one tough guy. Great issues and values worth dying for, worth living for, do exist—faithfulness, integrity, courage, determination, purpose, and love (just to name a few).

Isabella bowed her head and wept, "To die will be awful."

Wallace whispered back, "Every man dies, not every man really lives." I want to be one of those men who "really lives"—a deep man in a shallow world.

Justin Taylor, an executive vice president for Crossway Publishing, commented on the life J. I. Packer, who recently died at age 93, "I can only add that in every single encounter I was privileged to have with him, I came away thinking of him not as a great man, but as a man who had personally encountered a Great Savior." Packer lived deeply.

At the end of my journey, when I have breathed my last and close my eyes for the last time, I want it said that I followed hard after those things that truly matter: Christlikeness above all; personal integrity; right living; genuine faith, mercy and forgiveness; love for God and others; and a stable and sure life in a world that has lost its moral compass and knows little of what matters. I want my life to showcase the positive, deep relationships cultivated to last a lifetime and beyond in my family, my neighborhood, my church, and ultimately with my God. That's what I want—to be a person who sees life from God's point of view and looks intently at the world through the *"mind of Christ"* (I Cor. 2:16). Paul wrote, *"Let his mindset become your motivation"* (Phil. 2:5, TPT). In other words, keep an eternal, biblical perspective (more on that later) because frankly, it doesn't get any deeper (or better) than that.

In the sixteenth century, the English explorer, Sir Francis Drake, is credited with penning the following words, though there is some question of authorship. Regardless, it is a timeless prayer, especially in these days of pandemics, riots, and world unrest. Thousands have died across the globe from wars and pestilence. Many have lost their jobs and careers, their homes, their cars and boats, their cable TV, gym memberships, and hair stylists. Everything we once thought so important, so critical, and so vital to living the "good life" is being stripped away, exposing the shallowness and transient nature of our positions and possessions. Life has been paired down to the basics—meaningful, intimate, deep relationships with God and people. Not much else really matters. Let this be the prayer of your heart:

Introduction

Disturb us, Lord, when
Our dreams have come true
Because we have dreamed too little,
When we arrived safely
Because we sailed too close to the shore.

Disturb us, Lord, when
With the abundance of things we possess
We have lost our thirst
For the waters of life.
Having fallen in love with life,
We have ceased to dream of eternity
And in our efforts to build a new earth,
We have allowed our vision
Of the new Heaven to dim.

Disturb us, Lord, to dare more boldly,
To venture on wider seas
Where storms will show your mastery.
Where losing sight of land,
We shall find the stars…[9]

May God help us to live deeply in a shallow world. "Disturb us, Lord…" We need to be deep people. Let's get to it!

Endnotes

[1] E. M. Bounds, *Power Through Prayer* (Ontario, Canada: Devoted Publishing, 2016), 5ff.

[2] Richard Foster, *Celebration of Discipline: The Path to Spiritual Growth*, 20th Anniversary Edition (New York: HarperCollins, 1998), 1.

[3] John Eldredge, *The Journey of Desire* (Nashville: Nelson Books) 1-8.

[4] David W. McCullough, *The Trivialization of God* (Colorado Springs: Navpress, 1995), 41.

[5] Kenneth Humphries, "An Examination of Discipleship," *Treasured Truth Today*, 2020 Newsletter, Retrieved from http://www.treasuredtruthtoday.org/main/21-sermons/articles/mastering-discipleship/104-an-examination-of-discipleship.

[6] Os Guinness, *The Call* (Nashville: W. Publishing Group, 2003), 4.

[7] Biography.com Editors, *William Wallace Biography*, A&E Television Networks, September 11, 2019, https://www.biography.com/military-figure/william-wallace.

[8] Anugrah Kumar, "J. I. Packer, author of 'Knowing God,' dies at 93," *Christian Post*, July 18, 2020, retrieved from https://www.christianpost.com/news/ji-packer-author-of-knowing-god-dies-at-93-237971/?fbclid=IwAR14tUbLI8mYYV7ZDe5owFAd-dWZKHWONJWu-aFSdRh1D_O8GaALR1Darco.

[9] Joshua Horn, "Francis Drake's Prayer: Fact or Fiction?" *Discerning History*, Nov 24, 2014. http://discerninghistory.com/2014/11/francis-drakes-prayer-fact-or-fiction/.

> *"Without proper self-evaluation, failure is inevitable."*[1]
>
> – John Wooden

Chapter 1

Personal Assessment— How Deep Am I?

THE FIRST TIME God spoke to man (before humanity screwed things up), God told him to *"be fruitful and multiply, and fill the earth, and subdue it"* (Gen. 1:28)—a mandate to be God's man (or woman) in the world: in our neighborhoods, in the corporate world, on the college campus, or on a street corner selling newspapers. From the start, we were destined to be His representatives in the place of His choosing (wherever that may be, the Garden of Eden or elsewhere), faithfully serving His interests and fulfilling a particular role God, in His wisdom, designed for each one of us. Regrettably, I've not always done an especially good job at carrying out what God wants for my life. I've squandered my chances one too many times. If I'm honest, I've fallen prey to what A.W. Tozer identified as "the most widespread and persistent problem to be found among Christians…the problem of retarded spiritual progress."[2] Undoubtedly, I am guilty of living a shallow life amid great opportunities.

Roberto Clemente, one of the finest baseball players ever to play the game, was flying to Nicaragua with food and medicine for hurricane victims, having already funded three other such flights to the Central American country to provide much-needed help and relief to those who had lost everything. Unfortunately, on this final trip the plane in which he was flying went down, leaving no survivors. Before he boarded that ill-fated flight, Clemente had told reporters, "If you have a chance to accomplish something that will make things better for people coming behind you and you don't do that, you are wasting your time on this earth."[3] I'm afraid I've done a lot of that—wasting my time, not taking full advantage of the opportunities God has given me to invest in people and His kingdom, falling short of being the man He wants me to be and doing what He wants me to do.

I have been satisfied with minimal vision, settling for lesser roles than the ones God desired for me to play in this world. I've done much less with the potential to give so much more. This common problem among flesh and blood is one I've seen numerous times in my own life and in the lives of so many others—a tragic waste of time and energy! Over the years, I've conveniently forgotten the teaching of Christ—*"To whom much has been given, much will be required"* (Luke 12:48, AMP)—and I have indeed been given much. In the words of Uncle Ben to Spiderman, "With great power, comes great responsibility."[4]

C.S. Lewis observed,

> We are half-hearted creatures, fooling about with drink and sex and ambition when infinite joy is offered to us, like an ignorant child who wants to go on making mud pies in a slum because he cannot imagine what is meant by the offer of a holiday at the sea. We are far too easily pleased.[5]

Personal Assessment—How Deep Am I?

The words of Lewis challenge me to take a closer look at my own life. Paul reminded Christians at Corinth who were struggling with moral and biblical values to *"Examine yourselves to see if your faith is genuine. Test yourselves"* (II Cor. 13:5, NLT). Two imperatives are issued here: 1) *"examine"* your life (for substance/nature) and 2) *"test"* it (for authenticity/validity). These commands are designed to confront and modify the attitudes and behavior of believers everywhere. So how deep am I anyway? This could get terribly personal.

Honestly, I must admit that at times I have often settled for little more than a few creature comforts along the way—a good dinner (for me, it's pizza), a nice car equipped with all the latest electronic gadgets (as if I really know how to use them), some stylish, brand-name clothing, a good haircut, and of course, those new Nike running shoes. I have more than one pair. I have even entertained the crazy thought of riding Dollywood's 21-story roller-coaster, the "Wild Eagle," in pursuit of a one-minute thrill. So thankful the insanity of that thought passed quickly.

Unfortunately, I've spent more time than I should have and an enormous amount of energy to improve my status and station in my professional career. I have worked feverishly to climb the "corporate ladder" in order to gain recognition and hopefully earn more shekels to build "bigger barns." I admit I haven't gotten extremely far in those pursuits, or at least not as far as I had hoped. Further, I craved being center stage, to be admired by others and to hear the fleeting applause of the crowd, whose cheers I have always found intoxicating. I have accumulated more trophies and plaques than I care to remember and hung them on my office wall to commemorate any number of athletic and academic awards and achievements. But they have all tarnished, and so has the momentary exhilaration that accompanied those successes. All of it has long since passed.

I've also tried hanging out with the "right" people—pursuing relationships with "important" individuals, the ones I once thought would make great friends and business partners and might serve to advance my standing and interests, only to find out later that they were mere mortals, proving themselves little more than untrustworthy, self-serving acquaintances. How disappointing. How shallow. How very naive.

There may not be anything inherently evil about any of these pursuits, but their lack of significance is troublesome, downright foolish, and certainly shortsighted…at best, an empty and superficial lifestyle. I have often thought that if that is all there is to my life (a pair of Nike shoes and a few pats on the back), then I am (with most of the rest of the world) a shallow, sorry, miserable, dissatisfied man to say the least. I have been "far too easily pleased!" Guilty as charged!

Therefore, reevaluating the focus of my life against the life Jesus lived day in and day out becomes necessary. He sets the pace for the rest of us. Of course honesty (something most of us find difficult to embrace) is required in this pursuit. Undoubtedly, help from the Spirit of God and a measure of guts will most certainly be required to get a "real look see" and complete the job effectively and thoroughly. The spirit may be willing, but the flesh is certainly weak.

The process of God's sticking His nose into my business can be a most unpleasant and deeply personal experience. I was reluctant at first to open myself up but have since put that resistance aside and earnestly prayed (more than once over the years)…"*Search me, O God, and know my heart! Try me and know my thoughts* (He already does)! *And see if there be any grievous way in me* (If I've got it, He'll find it), *and lead me in the way everlasting*" (Psalm 139:23-24, ESV). Inviting God to rummage around every corner and crevice of my mind and heart is always a dangerous (but much needed) prayer. There is no telling what will pop up!

David wrote, *"O Lord, You have searched me and known me… and are intimately acquainted with all my ways"* (Psalm 139:1, 3). That phrase *"intimately acquainted"* is unsettling. It means that He flat-out knows me, and He knows me better than I know myself—everything is visible before Him, "the good, the bad, and the ugly." I am not a surprise or a mystery to God. Actually, no one is. *"All things are open and laid bare to the eyes of Him with whom we have to do"* (Heb. 4:13). Imagine for just a minute He knows what makes me (and you) tick, what I like, what I detest, what I want, and more importantly, what I need. There is no escaping His holy gaze. The Hound of Heaven can sniff out things I didn't even know were there. I cannot and should not hide.

> I fled Him, down the nights and down the days;
> I fled Him, down the arches of the years;
> I fled Him, down the labyrinthine ways
> Of my own mind; and in the mist of tears
> I hid from Him, and under running laughter.
> Up vistaed hopes I sped…
> From those strong Feet that followed, followed after.
> But without hurrying chase,
> And unperturbèd pace,
> Deliberate speed, majestic instancy…
> Across the margent of the world I fled…
>
> And pulled my life upon me; grimed with smears,
>   I stand amid the dust of the mounded years—[6]
>   – Francis Thompson, 1893

If the goal is to live more deeply, then I must of necessity place my life alongside the mind, heart, and actions of Christ, the One Who lived life to perfection. The comparison between His life and mine may prove to be a brutal assault on my pride but will be decisively revealing and hopefully life-changing. I suspect I may not fare so well in this analysis. When all is said and done, I will fall short of the holy standard along with the rest of humanity.

The gospel of John provides an overview of just how Jesus lived His life and what motivated Him to do the things He did. As He moved through the day and interacted with people, He set the highest of standards for living deep in this world—a standard against which I must measure my own attitudes and actions. Nothing less will do, not if I'm looking to go deeper with God and have any shot at living life as it's meant to be. Divine probing must take place. A little divine interrogation goes a long way.

The hard questions that follow are not meant to be exhaustive but are based on the life and ministry of Christ, as seen in John's Gospel. They are designed to provide a basic understanding for daily Christian practice. Get set to be a bit uncomfortable as the holy inquiry begins.

- Do I recognize the authority of God over all areas of my life (5:43; 8:42), or am I looking elsewhere for validation and approval?

- Am I fully committed to do the will of God in all matters (4:34; 5:30; 6:38), or am I more dedicated to my own ideas, ambitions, and personal agenda?

- Does my life reflect consistent compliance with God's Word (5:17), or am I independent, autonomous, defiant, and selective in my daily choices?

Personal Assessment—How Deep Am I?

- Do I have a clear understanding of my identity—who I am and what I am supposed to be doing in the world (8:14), or have I forfeited my rights and potential as a son or daughter of God?

- Am I impacting my culture and generation with the truth of the gospel (7:7), or have I lost my moral reference and footing?

- Do I possess a thorough, working knowledge of the Word of God, making it central to all my decisions and actions (8:26; 12:49-50), or do I settle for *"the traditions of men"* or another *"empty philosophy"* (Col. 2:8) to guide my daily life?

- Do I live undeterred and determined to carry out God's plan for my life no matter what it may cost (8:12), or am I willing to travel a more popular, broader, easier road, and go the *"way which seems right to a man"* (Prov. 14:12)?

- Do I understand the purpose of God for my life (8:14, 29), or do I see another alternative that drives me forward?

- Am I living daily in light of the presence of God (8:29; 16:31), or do I face the day resisting God's influence and intervention in my life?

- Have I developed a personal, intimate relationship with God the Father (8:55), or have I found someone or something else I consider to be of greater importance and significance?

- Is my love for God demonstrated by my obedience to God (14:31), or do I give God lip service when asked to follow His commands?

- Am I glorifying/honoring God in attitude and action (8:49; 12:28; 17:4), or am I more interested in shameless self-promotion and self-interest?

- Am I living life as a testimony to the reality of God so others might see Him more clearly (17:26), or am I guilty of obscuring the reality and truth of God and His will by the way I live?

So how did I (you) measure up? As one might expect, a good deal of work remains to be done in all our lives. Surprise, surprise! I have not arrived (and you haven't either) at the pinnacle of Christian living. Like most people trying to follow Christ, nearly everything about my personal and spiritual life needs improvement and attention. It seems there is always room for further progress. C.S. Lewis concluded:

> The job (of fully maturing in Christlikeness) will not be completed in this life: but He [God] means to get us as far as possible before death. That is why we must not be surprised if we are in for a rough time.[7]

Paul instructed the believers in Ephesus to *"be imitators of God* (a rather tall order for flesh and blood) *...learn what is pleasing to the Lord"* (Eph. 5:1, 10). That about sums up deep living—*"learning"* to model Christ. Think like Him. Live like Him. Love like Him from the moment "newness of life" begins until the day you breathe your last breath and enter glory. It is how God intended life to be on planet Earth.

I'm still working at it. I am still hopeful. I am still positive for *"I have been crucified with Christ; and it is no longer I who live, but Christ lives in me..."* (Gal. 2:20). Christ in us is the only way the Christian life gets done. That is the secret to living deep: Christ doing what only He can do—living His life through my life. We will be better for it. We'll do better and live deeper. Take another look, and let God do His work His way in you.

Endnotes

[1] Jr Inman, *When the Air Comes Out of the Ball,* (Bloomington, Ill.: Author House, 2012), 35.

[2] A.W. Tozer, *The Root of the Righteous* (Chicago: Moody, 1986), 13.

[3] Brad Meltzer, Heroes for My Son, (New York: Harper Collins), 12-13.

[4] *Spider-Man,* directed by Samuel Raimi (April 29, 2002; Los Angeles: Columbia Pictures, May 2002) DVD.

[5] C. S. Lewis, *The Weight of Glory and Other Addresses,* ed. Walter Hooper (New York: Simon and Schuster), 25-26.

[6] D. H. S. Nicholson and A. H. E. Lee, *The Oxford Book of English Mystical Verse* (Oxford: At the Clarendon, 1917).

[7] C. S. Lewis, *The Complete C. S. Lewis Signature Classics,* (New York: HarperCollins, 2002), 162.

> *"And I entered and beheld with the eye of my soul...the Light Unchangeable...He that knows the Truth, knows what that Light is; and he that knows it, knows Eternity."*[1]
>
> – Saint Augustine

Chapter 2

Eternity on My Eyeballs

A.W. Tozer warned of *The Dangers of a Shallow Faith* when he wrote the following:

So my Christian friend, if you are settling back, snuggling in your rubber chair, and resting in your faith in John 3:16 and the fact that you accepted Jesus Christ, you had better watch yourself. Take heed; lest you also be found wanting. Take heed of your own heart lest that when all is said and done, you have become tied to the world.[2]

How unnerving—"tied" to a world that is solely concentrated on the trivial and the temporal. A pointless existence, no doubt, "when all is said and done." Everything within the realm of our daily experience is transient. Nothing is stable or secure. Everything changes and not always for the better, a lesson society has become more painfully aware of during the recent Coronavirus pandemic and the collapse of the Market to its worse levels since the Great Depression. Millions have lost jobs, personal income, retirement savings, position, and power—the very foundations upon which so many have built their futures. They have all fallen away in the blink of an eye, leaving behind little more than a shallow life, incapable of providing peace of mind, lasting satisfaction, or a deeper sense of purpose and meaning beyond the immediate.

Paul Tripp described his own experience of living in a superficial environment, wanting more out of life but getting so little (a common problem for us all).

> I long for
> Justice
> Love
> Hope
> Peace
> Perfection
> Satisfaction
> Mercy
> Contentment
> Rest
> Harmony
> Joy
> and none of these
> longings
> ever gets fully
> satisfied.
> And so in my quest

> for more
> I am faced with
> the incontrovertible
> daily evidence
> that this simply is not all
> that there is
> and the sure truth
> that I was
> hardwired
> for another world.³

If I'm going to live more deeply in such an insecure world, I must have a better view of *"another world,"* for which it seems I am better suited. Moses compared *"the momentary enjoyment of sin's pleasures…*[and what] *the world could offer him"* in the here and now (Heb. 11:25, TPT) against the surpassing value of faithfully serving Christ and His kingdom. He chose Christ, *"for his eyes looked with wonder not on the immediate, but on the ultimate—faith's great reward!"* (Heb 11:26, TPT). That reward is eternity lived out in the presence of God. Apparently, living in the grand palaces of Egypt was nothing in comparison to what God had in store for His man and his "forever and forever" future. I cannot seem to fully wrap my mind around the idea of *"from everlasting to everlasting"* (cf. Psalm 103:17). It doesn't quite compute.

"*The world* [and its philosophy of life]," John reminds us, "*is passing away, and the lust of it* [desires, cravings] *but he who does the will of God abides forever*" (I John 2:17, NKJV). Like so many, I had become accustomed to *"fooling about"* with lesser pursuits and minimal, temporary pleasures. It's about time that I (and you, too) begin to approach life differently and make the necessary adjustments.

Jonathan Edwards challenged me with a simple, yet profound prayer: *"Lord, stamp eternity on my eyeballs."* A good way to start the day, looking at life from an eternal perspective, means that all my thoughts, emotions, failures, achievements, circumstances, relationships, and actions (insignificant or otherwise) must be carefully calculated and considered beyond the immediate moment. Eternity is always to remain in view—the lens through which all things must be seen and assessed, from the happiest moments to the most tragic events, from the shedding of tears in the night to the promises of joy in the morning (Psalm 30:5), from the tragedy of the cross to the victory of the empty tomb. Somehow, every event and aspect of my life fits marvelously together, like a thousand-piece puzzle, into God's grand scheme, conceived in eternity past, *"before the foundation of the world"* (Eph. 1:4).

Paul wrote to the believers at Colossae, *"Set your mind on the things above"* and not on this earth (cf. Col. 3:1-2). In other words, take a good, hard look at where your life is headed in the long run. What's the end game? When Jesus asked, *"What does it profit a man if he gains the whole world and loses his soul?"* He made clear the importance of moving through the day (and every day) with eternity in view because the choices we make and the actions we take in any given moment will, in fact, define tomorrow.

That perspective is key for making a positive difference, not only in your own daily life but also in the lives of the people around you, right where you live, right now, impacting your home, family, workplace, school, church, community, and neighborhood. That's what deep people do—live well and move with divine intent and an eternal purpose until the day ends and they step through the doorway of eternity. They know what is important to God and so focus their efforts today with an eye set toward tomorrow and all the tomorrows to come.

That viewpoint comes only from God's written revelation and the guiding influence of the *"Spirit of truth,"* Who will be *"with you forever"* (John 14:16-17, NIV). And there it is again, life with a *"forever"* point of view—living out God's eternal truth, serving His eternal interests, impacting the lives of others both now and for all time. That's a perspective deep people develop and maintain. "What we do in life [certainly] echoes in eternity."[4]

Two thousand years ago Seneca, the Roman philosopher, observed how most people lived in his generation—wasting precious time, living shortsighted without the slightest thought of tomorrow. Actually, it all sounds so terribly modern, so relevant to our current culture and world. He said,

> You live as if you were destined to live forever (on this earth), no thought of your frailty ever enters your head, of how much time has already gone by, you take no heed. You squander time as if you drew from a full and abundant supply, though all the while that day…is perhaps your last.[5]

Some things just don't seem to change.

Job's friends reminded him that today is not forever. *"Our days on earth,"* they said, *"are but a shadow"* (Job 8:9, NIV). That may be the understatement of the ages! David prayed,

> *Lord, remind me how brief my time on earth will be. Remind me that my days are numbered—how fleeting my life is* (Ps. 39:4, NLT).

Today is here and gone all too quickly. The days pass. The holidays roll on by. The birthdays come and go. From the dust we came, and soon (too soon) to the dust we shall return. Our lives are but *"a wind that passes and does not return"* (Ps. 78:39) and that makes time (while we've got it) precious since it cannot be renewed or recovered. Frankly, there is no time to lose. We have but a few moments here. "Where," I ask, "did that young man go who used to be in the mirror?"

That same sense of urgency is common among those living deep in a shallow world. They *"walk not as unwise men, but as wise, making the most of* [their] *time"* (Eph. 5:15-16), living with few regrets and taking *"full advantage of every day as you spend your life for his purposes"* (Eph. 5:16, TPT). Shallow people do otherwise. They live only for the moment and forget tomorrow. The writer to the Hebrews issued a final reminder, if not a warning, to all. *"It is appointed for man to die once, and after that comes judgment"* (Heb. 9:27, ESV).

The typical lifespan is some seventy-five years (give or take a few). For you mathematicians, we spend nearly twenty-five of those years in bed sleeping (and some much more than that, it seems), snoozing away our lives! That's a third of every day, every month, every year engaged in seemingly unproductive activity (except for the health benefits of adequate sleep), accomplishing so little in this world. There is not much time left to get on with life and perhaps do something of significance in our marriage, family, career, and relationships.

If we fail to recognize the brevity of our situation and the reality of eternity, the tendency will be to drive our *"tent pegs"* down too deeply into the shifting sands of earthly life—a potentially costly mistake. Life is short. Eternity (a long, long time) is unending and fast-approaching, looming on the horizon, and no replays are permitted in life (except on ESPN). David said to his friend, *"There is hardly a step between me and death"* (I Sam 20:3), and so it was for David as it is for us—a reason to let an eternal perspective dominate my thinking and guide my actions. *"Lord, stamp eternity on my eyeballs"* because the ultimate goal

Eternity on My Eyeballs

at the end of the race when this life has come to a close is *"the prize of the upward call of God in Christ Jesus"* (Phil. 3:14). That focus is clearly needed every moment of every day. Deep people get it…and live their lives accordingly.

In light of eternity, Edwards laid out the following resolutions for his personal life.

- Resolved, never to lose one moment of time; but improve it the most profitable way I possibly can.
- Resolved, never to do anything, which I should be afraid to do, if it were the last hour of my life.
- Resolved, that I will live so as I shall wish I had done when I come to die.
- Resolved, to ask myself at the end of every day, week, month and year, wherein I could possibly in any respect have done better. Jan. 11, 1723.
- I frequently hear people in old age say how they would live, if they were to live their lives over again: Resolved, that I will live just…as I shall wish I had done, supposing I live to old age. July 8, 1723.
- Resolved, to endeavor to my utmost to act as I can think I should do, if I had already seen the happiness of heaven, and hell's torments. July 8, 1723.[6]

That's deep! Eternity impacts and changes how we decide to live each day—or at least it should. Spurgeon said, "The best moment of a Christian's life is his last one, because it is the one that is nearest heaven. And it is then that he begins to strike the keynote of the song which he shall sing to all eternity."[7]

An Ordinary Day

This is one of those tough
   Tedious days.
An ordinary day, actually.
   A day of testings,
Annoying disturbances,
   Unscheduled disruptions,
Relentless pressures.
   Endless tension.

Nevertheless,
   It is the only day I've got.
Yesterday cannot be retraced.
   Tomorrow has yet to arrive.
This day is mine,
   This day alone.
And with it,
   Uncharted frontiers await,
Immeasurable possibilities,
   Great potential.
Intertwined with dull routines,
   Daily blunders,
And little mishaps
   Granted by God.
The thought settles me.
   Subdues me.
Provokes me.

Eternity on My Eyeballs

No doubt,
   The day belongs to me.
I am responsible for it.
   Every minute.
Every hour.
  To do.
     To create.
        To be.
To explore.
    To experience.
       To fill.

Now,
   I can make something happen
In the course of this ordinary day,
   Despite the tyranny of the moment.
I can *"make level paths for my feet"* (cf. Heb. 12:13).
   I can learn.
     I can trust.
        And I can grow.

Or I can resign to failure.
   Cave in to discouragement.
Collapse under disillusionment.
   And sink down in self-pity.
A victim of circumstances.
   Helpless.
     Hopeless.
       Hapless.

And so, end the day drained.
   Emptied of all reserve,
      All resolve.

The choice is mine.
   I will decide about today.
I will determine the outcome.
   "Choose you this day whom you
      Will serve!"
Such is the call of God in Christ Jesus.
   It is the power and privilege
To make things happen,
   To choose life, not death,
To live with eternity in view!
   It is an invitation to transform
An Ordinary Day
   Into an EXTRAORDINARY one![8]

Endnotes

[1] "Jesus, Socrates, and the Problem of Human Blindness," *The Front Porch Philosopher*, March 22, 2018, retrieved from https://thefrontporchphilosopher.com/2018/03/22/jesus-socrates-and-the-problem-of-human-blindness/.

[2] A.W. Tozer, *The Dangers of a Shallow Faith* (Bloomington, Minn.: Bethany House, 2012), 15.

[3] Paul Trip, "Made for Another World," *Articles/Post,* March 3, 2015, https://www.paultripp.com/articles/posts/made-for-another-world.

[4] *Gladiator,* directed by Ridley Scott (2000; Los AngelesDreamWorks, Universal Pictures, and Scott Free Productions, 2000), DVD.

[5] "Who Is Seneca? Inside the Mind of the World's Most Interesting Stoic," *Daily Stoic*, Retrieved from https://dailystoic.com/seneca/.

[6] Matt Perman, "The Resolutions of Jonathan Edwards," *Desiring God*, Dec 30, 2006, https://www.desiringgod.org/articles/the-resolutions-of-jonathan-edwards.

[7] "Charles Spurgeon on Eternity, *Christian Quotes,* http://christianquotes.ochristian.com/christian-quotes_ochristian.cgi?find=Christian-quotes-by-Charles+Spurgeon-on-Eternity.

[8] Sanford Zensen, "An Ordinary Day," *The Alliance Monthly*, Oct 14, 1987.

> "*The loneliest moment in life is when you have just experienced that which you thought would deliver the ultimate, and it has just let you down.*"[1]
>
> – Ravi Zacharias

Chapter 3

WHAT REALLY COUNTS

ONE DAY MY five-year-old son decided it was a good idea to park his bike (with the training wheels still attached) suspended over a mud puddle. I was watching him from a window inside our home when he started pedaling for all he was worth, as fast as he could, but he was not moving. Mud was flying everywhere. He was laughing and giggling, and his friends were cheering him on. *"Keep going. Don't stop!"* They were having a great time, the most fun of the day. It wasn't long before his face, hair, and clothes were covered with dirt and mud. He was quite a sight. His mother, of course, refused to let him back into the house until I first hosed him off and stripped him down.

I was amused at the whole event and couldn't help smiling, but later I thought that this was a perfect picture of how life looks when it is lived apart from Christ, without purpose and meaning—spinning our wheels. We get to pedaling as hard as we can through daily life, but we end up covered in dirt and mud, going nowhere fast, accomplishing so very little. Such is the plight of shallow men and women.

Ruth Paxson, in her classic *Life on the Highest Plane*, remarked,

> Many Christians do not seem to be conscious of their lack or their need. They are indifferent and self-satisfied…there are (also) many whose lives are characterized by a humiliating consciousness of defeat and failure, by a growing unrest, and by a perpetual striving for something never attained. Their hearts cry out insistently, "Lord, is there nothing better than this for me in the Christian life?"[2]

This honest question demands an immediate response. Of course, there is so much more I have yet to experience in my journey with Christ. A deeper life and a closer walk with Him are absolute musts if I'm ever going to figure this thing out called life and experience the best He has to offer.

Unfortunately, I have often lost sight of what truly matters and Who truly satisfies—and that, most certainly, is God Himself! Intimacy with Him is what really counts, actually the only thing that genuinely counts in the end. Everything else, suggested the apostle Paul, is *"rubbish"* (Phil 3:8—*skybalon*, meaning "dung" or "garbage"). Any way you cut it, that's pretty strong language. Paul was convinced that knowing *"Christ Jesus my Lord"* experientially and personally is of *"surpassing value."* In other words, there is nothing better or of more importance. He believed a deep relationship with Christ tied every believer to the redemptive *"power of His resurrection and the fellowship of His sufferings"* (cf. Phil 3:8-10). I like the *"power"* part—but not so keen on the *"suffering"* end of things.

I know, however, that living through those tough, hard days that often accompany life in a fallen world is a necessary part of the Christian life, producing the greatest growth in faith and Christlikeness. Frankly, I've never learned anything of substance at a party, only on the cutting edge of life where I have found Christ in the thick of difficult, trying circumstances—the One Who is *"before all things, and in him all things hold together"* (Col.1:17, NIV), and that, I might quickly add, includes the holding together of my personal life.

Having a deep relationship with God is highly satisfying. It takes me through the day (no matter how good or bad it gets) and fulfills the deepest longings of the human soul like no one or nothing else can. And that's what counts. A deep man or woman is ultimately satisfied with God in Christ Jesus. Blaise Pascal, the mathematician, philosopher, and theologian of another generation (1623-1662) concluded,

> What else does this craving, and this helplessness, proclaim but that there was once in man a true happiness, of which all that now remains is the empty print and trace?
>
> This he tries in vain to fill with everything around him, seeking in things that are not there the help he cannot find in those that are, though none can help, since this infinite abyss can be filled only with an infinite and immutable object; in other words by God himself. God alone is man's true good.[3]

A number of years ago, I met a well-known NBA basketball player (can't reveal his name), one of the finest who had ever laced up a pair of high-top, B-ball sneakers. He'd had a remarkable career, played for championship teams, and was still going strong playing with some of the game's very best. We met at a hospital where he was visiting his wife who was a patient at the facility. She was struggling from apparent spousal abuse, and he was feeling guilt and remorse over the events that had taken place. We were walking together across the campus when he asked me if I knew who he was. I did not recognize him at first, but when he told me his name, I was able to "put the pieces of the puzzle together." We started talking about life in general and his own personal journey. Over the course of our conversation, he made a stunning, though honest, admission. I'll never forget what he said:

> I worked hard to succeed in athletics—devoted an extraordinary amount of time to make it. I thought it was what I wanted. But when I got there [to the pro ranks]—to the top of the game with all the fame, fortune, status, and all that came with success, I found it was empty, and it did not satisfy.

He would have fared better had he connected with God earlier in his life and given Christ *"first place in everything"* (cf. Col. 1:16-18) rather than live without a clear sense of what was truly important in the long haul. His entire approach to daily living was marred and lacking substance. His marriage, values, and career were drastically skewed in the wrong direction. D. L. Moody said, "Let God have your life; He can do more with it than you can."[4]

The difference the Word and the presence of God can make in a person's life is nothing short of miraculous—be it on the shores of the Red Sea, at the walls of Jericho, in a prison with the apostles, or in a Roman arena facing wild beasts. In one instance, you find *"true wealth"* (Heb. 11:26, TPT). In the opposite scenario, you will be singing with the likes of Mick Jagger, "I Can't Get No Satisfaction,"[5] which may be the classic theme song of those living superficially in the world. A life void of God brings no deep, lasting contentment. *"All is vanity,"* so said the wisest and perhaps wealthiest man (Solomon) who ever walked this planet (Eccl. 1:2). King Solomon summed up how life was best meant to be lived—*"Fear God and keep His commandments"* (Eccl. 12:13). That admonition puts everything in perspective.

Several years ago I spoke with a highly successful and admired attorney who had risen to the top of his professional game. Well respected and well connected, he had made a boatload of money, owning two beautiful homes, several late model cars, a closet full of fashion suits, designer shoes, expensive watches, and everything else affluence and privilege he could afford to buy. He spent much of his spare time at the Blackjack tables in Atlantic City, looking for the next "big score." He lost multiplied thousands.

One day we stood outside his home in the hot summer sun and talked about life in general. We spoke of purpose, meaning, and values. I recall his "closing argument" that summed up his entire life philosophy. "Sandy," he said, *"the only thing that really matters in this life is to accumulate as many trinkets and toys as possible while you can, because when you die that's all there is. Nothing else. Zero. It's over. So go get it and enjoy it now while you can."* Empty words from a superficial man living a basically meaningless existence.

David, the shepherd boy who rose to be king, walked the halls of a palace and enjoyed the privilege of position, power, and money. He suggested that life, if it's going to work, should focus on something deeper and more satisfying—*"Make God the utmost delight and pleasure of your life, and he will provide for you what you desire the most"* (Psalm 37:4, TPT). The word *make*, also translated *delight*, is an imperative and means "to take one's pleasure in." *The Message* translates the verse: "Keep company with God, get in on the best." Good advice. A life centered in God alone as the ultimate source of one's strength and joy is the heart of living deep in a shallow and unstable world. When life goes south (and it will at some point) and the mountains shake and the seas roar, men will fall to their knees in the streets, stand on hospital rooftops, lift their hands toward heaven (observed on the nightly news during the Covid-19 pandemic), pleading for God to step in and rescue and save. Living deep is how we *"get in on [God's] best."*

In the 1981 movie *Chariots of Fire,* Harold Abrahams, a 1924 British Olympic sprinter, was asked prior to the 100-meter race why he trained and ran. His response was telling. He sighed, searching for a satisfying answer.

> Contentment. I'm 23 and I've never known it. I'm forever in pursuit, and I don't even know what it is I'm chasing…I'll raise my eyes and look down that corridor four-feet wide, with ten lonely seconds to justify my whole existence…but will I?[6]

Abraham was the antithesis of Eric Liddell, the missionary-bound young man, who refused to run the 100-meter race because the contest fell on a Sunday, his day of worship. The "Flying Scotsman" (that's what they called him) held tightly to deep convictions. Later in the games, Eric won a gold medal and set an Olympic record in the 400-meter race, an event he had never run before. He then left to serve the Lord in the South Pacific, ending up in a small mission camp during WWII. He fed and sheltered people ravaged by the war and served those helpless souls incarcerated in a Japanese prison, dying in that forsaken place a few years later as he ministered to and loved on people.

When Liddell raced, he had a simple plan that reflected the manner in which he lived his life—committed and dependent upon God. He said, *"The secret of my success over the 400m is that I run the first 200m as fast as I can. Then, for the second 200m, with God's help, I run faster."*[7]

Stephen Metcalf, a fellow internee at the prison camp, later wrote of Liddell, *"He gave me two things. One was his worn-out running shoes, but the best thing he gave me was his baton of forgiveness. He taught me to love my enemies, the Japanese, and to pray for them."*[8]

Eric Liddell was a deep man. He learned to dig deeper and live deeper than most. Abrahams, on the other hand, never did find contentment and the justification for his existence. He never went deep enough.

One night I received an unexpected call from John, one of my former collegiate soccer players. He and his wife (I had the privilege of officiating their wedding) were in town. It had been years since his graduation. John was a wonderful young man who loved the Lord and loved His Word. He asked if they could stop in for a short visit. It was late Sunday night, so I almost said no. I'd had a long week and I was tired, but I invited them to the house anyway. They arrived a little after 9 p.m. We talked, laughed, and reminisced about days gone by. It was good to be together again, especially since I had spent a good deal of time with John while he was at college. He was now teaching Bible and coaching varsity soccer at a Christian school in the Atlanta area and had returned to Dayton, Tennessee, for the weekend to speak to the youth in one of the local churches where he had ministered during his college days.

He asked, "Coach, do you remember what you said to me, what you told me?"

I quickly responded, "John, do I have to eat my words?"

He simply smiled and said in a soft voice, "No." and went on. "Remember the day when we got to talking about my future and what God wanted me to do with my life? You told me that God was looking for a man who would spend his life investing in people because that was what Jesus did and that there was no better way to live one's life. I am here to tell you that I took your advice. God found his man, and I'm doing just that...and I love it."

Shortly after his visit, John died suddenly of a heart attack while playing with his dog in the backyard of his home. He was only thirty-two years old. I was glad for those few precious moments we spent together that Sunday evening. Though his years seemed, from a human perspective, to have been cut short, he lived out his days fruitfully, faithfully, and fervently, serving the interests of Christ and His kingdom. It was obvious that he *"loved it."* He lived with eternity ever before him and found it deeply satisfying.

Tim Tebow once said, "Regardless of whatever I do, I know what my purpose is: to make a difference in people's lives."[9] John did just that. He was a man who lived well in a shallow world, living life as God intended. That's what counts. We need a few more men and women just like that!

Endnotes

[1] Cheri Fuller and Jennifer Kennedy Dean, *The One Year Praying the Promises of God* (Carol Streams, Ill.: Tyndale House, 2012), 89.

[2] Ruth Paxson, *Life on the Highest Plane* (Chicago: Moody, 1928), 9.

[3] Thomas V. Morris, *Making Sense of it All: Pascal and the Meaning of Life* (Grand Rapids: William B. Eerdmans, 1992), 134.

[4] Billy Graham, *Unto the Hills: A Daily Devotional* (Nashville: Thomas Nelson, 2010), July 17.

[5] Mick Jagger, vocalist, "I Can't Get No Satisfaction," by Mick Jagger and Keith Richards, recorded May 1965, *Out of Our Heads,* London Records, vinyl LP.

[6] *Chariots of Fire*, directed by Hugh Hudson (October 9, 1981, Paris, Warner Brothers, 1981) DVD.

[7] *Chariots of Fire*.

[8] Steve Metcalf, *Eric Liddell's Baton*, https://www.ericliddell.org/stephen-a-metcalf/.

[9] Tim Tebow Quotes. *BrainyQuote.com,* BrainyMedia Inc, 2020. https://www.brainyquote.com/quotes/tim_tebow_735482, accessed September 3, 2020.

> *I drown in grief. "I'm heartsick.*
> *Oh, listen! Please listen! It's the cry of my dear*
> *people reverberating through the country...*
> *For my dear broken people, I'm heartbroken.*
> *I weep, seized by grief.*
> *Are there no healing ointments in Gilead?*
> *Isn't there a doctor in the house?*
> *So why can't something be done*
> *to heal and save my dear, dear people?"*
> – Jeremiah (8:18-22, MSG)

Chapter 4

Let My Heart Be Broken

As we stood on the sidelines during pre-game, one of the most successful collegiate coaches in the United States told me that his personal life over the last six months had deteriorated into a disaster. It had been a year since I had seen him last.

During his career, the man had reached the height of the coaching profession, highly decorated with multiple national "Coach of the Year" awards and numerous championships to his credit. His teams were consistently ranked in the top five in the country. He had it all: position, prestige, awards, success. But it wasn't enough. It never is.

His facial expressions told the story. He was a miserable, dejected, and discouraged man. I asked him what was going on. His wife had walked out the door with two of his three children after twenty-five years of marriage. She packed up and split, the family unit dissolved. She later filed for divorce, and he was left to wallow in self-pity and an empty house. The marriage was over.

Frankly, his wife didn't want to deal with the late nights any longer, wondering when her husband would be home from the frequent recruiting trips that left her alone and anxious for long stretches of time. No more. Enough. This was going to end. She refused to stand by and watch the neglect of her children by their father, the broken promises, the emotional distance, the lack of servant-leadership, and his apparent disinterest in building and maintaining a strong, intimate relationship with his wife, the woman who was supposed to be the most important person in his life. She never was, at least not in their later years. He admitted,

> You know, I wasn't home much. I spent my time and energy out here on the field, traveling, building my program, but not building my family. She had had enough. Our relationship was destroyed—my family is torn apart, and I hurt so bad.

I could see it in his eyes—empty, hopeless, distant, dead on the inside—the results of shallow living and the subsequent death of his marriage. He clearly mourned his loss, and my heart broke for him. The anguish and heartache of a man with little hope and a ton of regrets is indescribable—hard to imagine, harder to see. He was desperate for relief. He needed healing and wholeness. He needed new life. *"I'm trying to recover,"* he said. *"I realized that if I'm ever going to make it, I need to make some changes and have God part of my life."*

I challenged him right then and there on the sidelines prior to the start of the contest. It seemed a little out of place, but I spoke up anyway. This was more important than winning or losing a game. This was life, his life. He needed answers, and he needed them now. I said,

> God does not simply want to be part of your life. That's not good enough. He must BE your life from the moment your feet hit the floor in the morning to the time you fall into bed at night. No holdouts. Divorce was not God's design, but He can use this tragedy to press you into making positive changes in your life and bring something good out of the mess you've made.

Pretty bold and direct, if you ask me. But this was no time to provide him an easy way out or offer him some psychological babble that softens moral responsibility and fails to demand a change of heart and behavior. A direct, "in-your-face" confrontation was necessary at this point. He needed a friend who cared enough to tell him what he *must* hear and not simply say what he *wanted* to hear. The former brings change; the latter fixes nothing. I learned many years ago that God is more interested in permanent healing than temporary relief.

I followed up the next day with an email to check on him. Here was his response, which left me amazed at the healing power of God. He wrote,

> Thank you so much for the follow-up and the time we spent last night. Even though it was very brief, it meant more than you know… My story is certainly a painful journey, but each day is getting better… My life has been very empty when I reflect on my relationship with the Lord. That is going to change.

Several days later he contacted me again. He had gotten involved in a

Bible study with a number of other men and was learning how to apply the truth of God's Word to his daily life. He acknowledged, *"I am beginning to see that there is so much more to life, and what a life I have missed out on. Never again..."* I rejoice to this day over the resurrection and salvation of a man dead in his sins. The outcome could have been very different had God not broken my heart and pressed me to speak truth into his life.

At the tomb of Lazarus (John 11), eyewitnesses reported that *"Jesus wept"* (v. 35) at the sight of the grave. He loved Lazarus (v. 36) and his family, but that was not the sole cause for His tears. John also recorded that Jesus was *"deeply moved in spirit and was troubled"* (v. 33), not just upset but downright enraged by what He saw. The tomb seemed so certain, so final, so real. His heart objected to what His eyes could not deny—the "sting" of death and a cold grave. He groaned at the sight.

Jesus then turned His attention back toward the crowd. Tears filled His eyes once again, coupled with divine, righteous anger that simultaneously erupted from within. Everything seemed so wrong—from the pain of Mary and Martha, sisters of the deceased, to their woeful cry of bewilderment. Death had claimed their precious brother. And like so many facing a similar loss, the women were devastated and confused, wondering where God was in all of this. Jesus saw clearly (He always does) what nobody else wanted to or could possibly see—just how far the depravity of man had gone and the hideous results of failing to live as God intended. He saw (and sees) everything: the loss of life, the end of hopes and dreams, and a future with its buried potential now gone forever. The sin of humanity has incredible destructive force. It kills. There is no getting around it. The wages of sin is always death. Living deep readily acknowledges that horrible fact. The consequences are unmistakable.

Nothing was/is hidden from the omniscient, eternal *"son of man"* (that's Jesus), Who is able to look out across the universe and see the lives of real people, every person who has ever lived or will live, and instantly track their every move from the cradle to the grave, even before their life unfolds. He saw the crippled man on a stretcher by the pool of Bethesda, the blind man on the side of the road, the ten lepers begging to be made whole, the frightened Shunammite woman whose son had died, the tax-collector who stole from his neighbors, a thirsty woman hauling water from a Samaritan well, the religious leaders and Jerusalem temple congregants, as well as pagans and heretics, prophets and kings, peasants, beggars, and prostitutes. *"The eyes of the* Lord *move to and fro throughout the earth"* (II Chron. 16:9), combing the annals of human history, privy to the abundance of moral failures, the countless abortions that rob the unborn of life, the drunk lying in the streets slowly drinking his/her life away, the drug dealers and their clients looking to score, the pimps who exploit young women, the rich and famous who never seem to be satisfied, and the Wall Street broker dressed in designer suits, cheating his way to the top.

Under the watchful eyes of the Divine, everything is magnified. God is no respecter of men. All have fallen short of God's standards of decency and morality and are paying a heavy price, desperately trying to make it in this world—attempting to succeed in some venture, attempting to do better…but not having much luck.

To this day, the world remains a tragic story of shallow thinking and shallow living. Nothing has changed. Nothing is the way God intended. Nothing is right. The Son of God still looks down from above through eyes filled with tears and a broken heart. He's seen it all, felt it all, and eventually carried it all—the emptiness, the sadness, the hopelessness, and the ruined lives—to a hill called Golgotha to redeem the lives of men and women everywhere. That's good news—great news!

Since the days Adam and Eve walked the lush garden paths of Eden, the landscape has been littered with fractured, discarded lives that have broken the heart of God. Like the garbage piled high in the Valley of Hinnom outside the walls of Jerusalem, the stench of human guilt and rotting lives overpowers the senses. It stinks. No wonder Jesus, *"a man of sorrows and acquainted with grief"* (Isaiah 53:3), *"wept bitterly."* Deep people cry too because they have seen life through the eyes of the Redeemer and cannot possibly remain the same or live the same. They just can't. They must act. They must approach life redemptively and be the men and women of God who will bring the reality of Christ's kingdom to their generation and to their little corner of the world.

Deep people want in on that story—to be a part of what God is doing in the world and to be used by Him in some meaningful way to let loose the healing presence of the Spirit of God on the human predicament, the brokenhearted for the broken. Like Jesus, deep people show up. Living out this profoundly personal matter, they feel deeply, speak truthfully, and act decisively, entering into humanity's pain with but one purpose: to bring the transforming, reconciling power of the gospel in order to redeem and rescue the lives of men and women.

The gospel is clear: God unselfishly threw off His royal robes, clothed Himself in human flesh, and left the palaces of Heaven *"to seek and to save"* a lost world. It doesn't get more personal than that. He did not, nor will He ever, sit idly by and let the thieves of hell *"steal, kill, and destroy"* (John 10:10, ESV) the lives of His children. Deep people will not let that happen without a fight.

Four days later, after the burial of Lazarus, words of hope flowed like *"living water"* from the mouth of the Savior, and grace was heard echoing across the cosmos and reverberating through the back-alley ways and streets of the ancient and modern worlds. A word from God Himself, the Giver of life, shouted loud and clear for all to hear. Mercy filled the air. The command was given. The dead were called to new life. *"Lazarus! Come forth!"* Three words released the *"power of God for salvation"* (Rom. 1:16), and out walked a dead man from a dark, cold tomb! From death to life. From sorrow to joy. Divine healing came. Rescue. Transformation. Liberty– the opportunity to live life as it was meant to be! It doesn't get any better than that. It doesn't get any deeper than that.

Jesus said to His disciples, *"I tell you this timeless truth: The person who follows me in faith, believing in me, will do the same mighty miracles that I do—even greater miracles"* (John 14:12, TPT). That sounds like a description of a deep person living in a shallow world.

World Vision's founder Bob Pierce looked out over a hurting world and saw hate-filled violence and the ravages of war, rampant hunger and disease, displaced children and broken homes. He later wrote these words in the flyleaf of his Bible: "Let my heart be broken with the things that break the heart of God."[1] His was a deep prayer of the soul offered by a deep person who walked daily with God, who recognized the great need of humanity, who stood ready to act in mercy, and who was poised to deliver with compassion the gospel message of hope and healing to a sick and dying world. *"The word of the cross…is the power of God"* (I Cor. 1:18, ESV).

One day while serving the local church, I went to visit a man in the hospital. He was the brother of one of my parishioners, and he was dying from the effects of years of drinking. His liver was shot, and his heart was cold. He was an angry man. Before I left my office, I prayed for God's wisdom and grace to prevail. I would later learn that I needed every bit of God's help.

When I arrived, the man cursed me vehemently. He used words I hadn't heard since my military days. He finally told me in no uncertain terms to get out of his room. He obviously did not want me there nor did he want to hear what I had to say. He had shut down. He was defiant, resentful, and agitated. I pressed him a bit further, but he dug his heels in even more. No breakthrough came, just resistance and opposition. Hell was fighting with all its demonic power to maintain its lethal hold on that man's soul and keep him chained to his despair. Finally, I'd had enough. My heart broke for this pitiful man who had ruined his life. I stepped to the foot of the bed, stared into his hate-filled eyes, and boldly called forth life from a man dead in his sins. I said pointedly,

> You are dying. You know it and I know it. What in the world are you holding on to in this world that is so important, so valuable, so precious that you can't let it go; you won't let go? What is of such importance, of such great value that you would turn down the greatest offer ever made to any man—and walk away from the mercy and love of God and God's forgiveness for the people you've hurt, for your past, your rebellious spirit, your self-destructive behavior, and your drinking that has robbed you of life, real life, a good life? In exchange for the mess you've made, God is offering you the free gift of eternal life and heaven? Why would you want to hold on to whatever you think you've got? You've got nothing left; you've been stripped of everything. Give what's left of your life to Christ. He will forgive you. He loves you and is waiting right now for you.

The man broke down and cried. He began to tell me about his dreadful past and how he had destroyed his life, hurt others, failed himself, and lived a life void of God. That afternoon a broken, shallow man came to the cross, where God, rich in mercy, breathed new life into his dead spirit. In that most holy of moments, a man in need of forgiveness for past wrongs received his pardon in Christ. He was released from a botched past. Mercy came, and the love of God miraculously lifted him out of his misery and hopelessness. The great hymn of the church still rings true: *"When nothing else could help, love lifted me!"*[2] The man's entire countenance immediately changed. Hate was replaced by love. Gratitude overwhelmed his bitterness. Peace settled a mind in absolute turmoil and fear. Hope replaced the weight of regret for lost years…and I witnessed it all. I am glad I was there.

In the end, that once-broken man who had cursed me threw his arms around my neck and begged me not to leave, asking me to please come back and visit again. I told him I would. Little did I know that God would require his soul that very night, calling him home. One day in eternity on streets of gold, I'm going to run into him again because God broke my heart and pressed me to deliver the life-giving message of the cross to a dying man. The gospel is *"salvation to everyone who believes"* (Rom. 1:16, NIV).

The church needs deep people who feel what God feels, see what God sees, and will do what God does—men and women with broken hearts, determined to be Jesus in a world of broken people.

> *Breathe on me, Breath of God,*
> *Fill me with life anew,*
> *That I may love what Thou dost love,*
> *And do what Thou wouldst do.*[3]

This hymn was written for those desiring to live deeply in a shallow world.

Endnotes

[1] Rich Stearns, "Blessed by a broken heart," *World Vision*, Aug 28, 2017, https://www.worldvision.org/hunger-news-stories/blessed-broken-heart.

[2] James Rowe and Howard E. Smith, "Love Lifted Me," *The Baptist Hymnal* (Nashville: Convention Press, 1991), 546.

[3] Edwin Hatch, "Breathe on Me, Breath of God," 241.

> *"We are not necessarily doubting that God will do the best for us. We are wondering how painful the best will turn out to be."*[1]
>
> – C. S. Lewis

Chapter 5

Settle Down

Faith is absolutely critical to the Christian life. It is the stuff from which courage is forged, supplying the ability and guts necessary to leave all life and death matters (down to the smallest of details) in the hands of a capable God. Faith is the means by which fear and anxiety are conquered, particularly when nothing seems to make sense, life seems out of control, and the prospects for the future look grim. These characteristics sound much like a typical day.

The need to go deeper with God and *"Let the peace of God rule in your hearts"* (Col. 3:15) is made evident every day of our lives. In short, if we have faith, we live in peace without fear and worry about those things (people and events) over which we have little to no influence. If we lack faith in a God, Who *"will take care of everything you need"* (Phil. 4:19, MSG), fear will dominate our thinking and cripple our ability to cope and succeed in this fallen world. We will be in for the fight of our lives.

Living Deep in a Shallow World

I will not ever forget the day of my granddaughter Madison's ACL surgery and the prayers that went up on her behalf. My wife and I traveled to the hospital to be with her mom and dad and await the doctor's report. To our relief, the medical procedure to repair the torn ligament was a success, but it did not end there. Rehab would begin immediately; a long hard, difficult year of recovery was ahead before she would be strong enough to step back on the basketball court to play the game she loved. Unfortunately, she tore her other ACL a year or so later and was forced to go through the process all over again. Needless to say, we were devastated. Another season gone, and the possibility of earning a future scholarship to play at the collegiate level, which was her dream, seemed all but lost.

I demanded an explanation from God (as if I could fully understand the end from the beginning of His plans). I was furious, nonetheless. Everything she had worked so hard for was now in jeopardy. At least, that was how I felt. No peace—in absolute turmoil, uncertain, and anxious for her well-being and her future. My faith was a train wreck and in many respects still is. I hurt so deeply, as she did. I needed to settle down, but I wanted answers first. What I got was a lesson.

On both days when Madison was injured, I had been seated in the stands. During the course of a pre-season summer basketball game, she took a hard blow to her knee, which knocked her to the floor. The pain was instant and intense, and I could see the tears flowing down her cheeks. The painful expression on her face told the story. Her father, the coach of the team, immediately came running out onto the floor, thinking the worst but hoping for better. I watched the drama unfold and saw Madison's father lovingly comfort his daughter. His words were soft and reassuring as he reached down with both hands and slowly helped her to her feet. With his strong arms draped around her, the two of them limped off, struggling to make it to the sidelines where the damage could be assessed and the process of healing could begin. The walk, which seemed to last an eternity, was agonizing for them and painful for those of us who watched.

In many ways the sight was pitiful, breaking my heart. But it was also a great reminder of my heavenly Father, Who sees my bruised and battered life, Who watches me being knocked down by any number of personal failures, foolish decisions, ruined relationships, the death of loved ones, all manner of diseases, and sometimes the malicious actions of others. The Father above sees my tears, hears my weeping, and is mindful of my broken heart, my discouragement, my uncertainty, and my fear of the future. He is the One Who rises up when I need Him (and I need Him even now as I pen these words), rushes to the aid of His hurting children, reaches down into the deep pit of despair, puts His compassionate, strong arms around me, lifts me up once more to my feet, and then, like a good Father, dusts me off and helps me move forward toward healing and wholeness. I have such a Father (so do you) Who runs to my rescue—a fact I would do well to remember when trouble arrives at my front door. I hope God gets here quickly because I need to settle down soon, trust Him a bit more with the unknown, and live deeper in this world of uncertainty and conflict.

The Assyrians were threatening the people of God. History tells us that Sennacherib, the Assyrian king (reigned 705-681 BC), was a strong military leader and a ruthless enemy. He had overrun the city of Lachish and slaughtered its inhabitants. Those who survived were chained and dragged off to slavery. He wanted Jerusalem next, the crown jewel of Judah, so he sent his own general and several other officials with a large army to the gates of the city to underline Sennacherib's challenge. The sight from the city walls must have been terrifying.

Hezekiah was under great pressure. He was anxious, apprehensive, and fearful of what might happen (remind you of anybody you know?) if he refused to capitulate to Assyrian demands for unconditional surrender. The Scriptures record that Hezekiah eventually brought the problem to God (a very good move in times of distress). *"He went up to the house of the LORD [the only place to go when trouble strikes]...And Hezekiah prayed... (Isa. 37:14-15) 'deliver us from his hand that all the kingdoms of the earth may know that You alone, LORD, art God'"* (Isa. 37:20). In short, Hezekiah simply told God about what was going on (as if He didn't already know). He appealed to a Higher Authority, and in so doing, he left the matter with the Most High—the God Whose reign and power stand forever over all (and that includes my troubles, trials, and uncertainties), the God Who made Heaven His throne and the earth His footstool (Isa. 66:1)—a fact deep people count on in their daily lives, particularly when trouble threatens.

Now that's a big God if you ask me. Actually, He needs to be that big to handle all of the things that come my way (and yours) and to ensure that what He wants to accomplish in the world (specifically in my personal life through all the ups and downs, heartaches, and joys) will be done. No army or COVID-19 virus or even multiple ACL injuries are going to stand in His way. The apostle Paul wrote,

> *I am convinced that nothing can ever separate us from God's love. Neither death nor life, neither angels nor demons,* **neither our fears for today nor our worries about tomorrow**—*not even the powers of hell can separate us from God's love* (Romans 8:38, NLT).

The extent and power of God's love comforts me, or at least it should. It calms my spirit and encourages my heart to know that God's desire and ability to rescue and save reaches me (and you) today, right where I live. He loved me yesterday. He loves me today. He will love me tomorrow. I can count on it. So can you. And that great love drives God to always bring His best to our daily lives, whether or not life unfolds immediately as we would desire. He does not change— forever the same from everlasting to everlasting. That is what the Scriptures teach. His presence and love know no end or boundaries. His love remains, intervening, interceding, and at times invading our personal space to accomplish His good will. Deep people build their lives on the love of God because real, *agapé*, action-oriented, divine love does not bail at the first sign of turbulence. God jumps in. He stays in. He enters into the fray of daily living. No exceptions.

Zephaniah reminded the people of God who were facing *"destruction and desolation…darkness and gloom"* (sounds like the nightly news) that *"The Lord your God is with you, he is mighty to save. He will take great delight in you, he will quiet you with his love, he will rejoice over you with singing"* (cf. Zeph. 3:15-17). A.W. Tozer wrote, *"While it looks like things are out of control, behind the scenes there is a God who has not surrendered authority."*[2] That's good to know when trouble is brewing. If I ever expect to live deeply in a shallow world, I had better get this issue of faith and the character of God straightened out. The two go together. Hezekiah quickly collected himself (no time to lose) and turned his attention in faith to trust God without hesitation or regret.

Jerusalem was surrounded, and the Assyrians were poised for the attack. The situation was dire with no possibility of escape. No good news anywhere. I could imagine sheer panic within the walls of the city and a massive run on toilet paper, hand sanitizer, and medical supplies. The supermarket shelves were probably empty, and the people were terrified for their families, their future, and their own lives. Normal life as they knew it was a thing of the past. But God countered. He always does. When He showed up as usual and unleashed *"the angel of the LORD,"* the Assyrians fell in utter defeat because one man in faith settled down and talked things over with God. That's what deep people do. Before the night ended, 185,000 of Assyria's crack troops were slain (cf. II Kings 19:31-36), and Sennacherib retreated with his tail between his legs.

Hezekiah had finally gotten the memo from the prophet: *"Do not be afraid because of the words that you have heard..."* (Isaiah 37:6)—a timely message for people living in a negative world besieged with a barrage of depressing reports. Bad news sells, but it doesn't produce hope or heal people in trouble. What does help is to remember God— that the promises of God are as sure and relevant today as they were three thousand years ago. That makes for good press and a good start to any day.

I got to thinking of something the "Duke," John Wayne, once said. I had it posted on the back side of my office door as a constant reminder. *"Courage is being scared to death but saddling up anyway."*[3] Insightful words. But there is a down side—for unless you know and trust God every day, you are not going to saddle up or go anywhere. Fear can paralyze the strongest of men. Jesus told His followers, especially Peter who would soon be running for his life, scared to death over what was going down in his neighborhood, *"Let not your heart be troubled. Believe in God, believe also in Me"* (John 13:38-14:1, NRSV). Apparently, the ability to handle well the events of the day is directly tied to believing deeply in God.

A student of mine recently wrote of the "hope of humanity"—that is, resting his future on man's ability to make progress and eventually make this world a better place, a place of peace, generosity, love, compassion, etc., etc. (sounds like the 60s to me or a Bob Dylan folk song). I suspect the young man had never opened his history books, read the front page of any newspaper, or watched the riots, looting, and destruction in the cities of America as recently reported on the national news.

Jesus was much more honest about humanity's weaknesses and limitations and more mindful of the downside of man's character and its potential consequences. *"He knew what was in each person's heart,"* and it wasn't pretty (cf. John 2:24-25, NLT). Just before His own arrest and crucifixion, He told His disciples that their lives would also fall apart. Hell was soon to break loose. He called it *tribulation, suffering, affliction* (John 16:33). Any way you translate it, the word means "trouble"—big trouble. We've all had our fair share of that.

As was His custom, the Lord spoke directly to the issue. He warned His disciples that under pressure they would all turn tail (not a very courageous bunch) and make a run for it to save their own skin. It wasn't just Peter who bailed. They all did. They all lost confidence in God and His purpose and plan for their lives and went their own way—back to the fishing nets they had once abandoned to follow Christ. Let's face it. The temptation to return to their former selves was strong, even as the desire to return to the mud pits of Egypt had once been. How very human. How very shallow. How very unsettling. How very me.

With little doubt, the depth of a man's faith shows when he is backed into a corner, when he is hurting the most, when he has come to the end of himself, has done everything he knows how to do, has run out of answers, and has nowhere else to turn. Then, and only then, does an individual find out what he/she really believes, what one's faith is truly made of—better yet, just how big his or her God is. In the darkest hour, faith is defined.

Tribulation always reveals the level and quality of my beliefs—

whether my personal faith amid life's difficulties is shallow or deep, fragile or solid, irrelevant or viable. A deep person trusts the wisdom and goodness of God (even when he doesn't understand it), knowing that God is working *His best for my best* in every circumstance, regardless of how painful it is at the moment or how troubling it may appear to be (Rom. 8:29).

Shallow living does otherwise. It takes God and God's love out of the picture and fails at every turn to account for the presence and influence of the God of Abraham, Isaac, and Jacob. While the presence of God is accompanied by the peace of God, the absence of the presence of God is accompanied by fear and anxiety. Surely a connection exists between trusting God and keeping one's head screwed on right and tight in turbulent times. Ask Moses and a bunch of unarmed slaves standing helpless on the shores of the Red Sea, facing six hundred of Egypt's finest war chariots closing in for the kill. Listen to the report of Joshua and Caleb who encouraged an army of former slaves to move forward and attack the giants of Canaan. Watch David face down a giant nobody else would dare challenge. Without a doubt, where my mind goes, the rest of me will follow. Obviously, faith matters if I'm going to live deeply.

Isaiah said of God,

You keep him [me] *in perfect peace* [and peace is what I need]
whose mind is stayed on you,
  because he trusts in you (Isa. 26:3, ESV).

A mind focused on God is key. His person, precepts, promises, provisions, plans, and power must stay in the forefront of our thinking, no matter how rough life may get or how well things might go. Living deep demands it. Never lose sight of God, because the quality of one's faith is dependent on the object upon which it rests. In other words: big God, big faith; little God, little faith. The closer I draw to God, the bigger He seems and the smaller everything else appears. A deep person needs but a glimpse of God to build a life of faith and thereby carry on successfully through the daily grind. Isaiah recorded exactly what God wanted His people to know about Himself. His words are a faith builder.

> *I am God, and there is no one like Me,*
> *Declaring the end from the beginning,*
> *And from ancient times things which have not been done,*
> *Saying, "My purpose will be established,*
> *And I will accomplish all My good pleasure"* (Isa. 46:10-11).

Clearly, nothing surprises God or causes the Creator of the universe to panic. He is sovereign overall. The will of God stands sure—an anchor for my troubled soul, a vital lesson the disciples learned in the midst of a fierce storm on the Sea of Galilee (Mark 4:35-41). You discover a lot about yourself and your faith when *"sorrows like sea billows roll."* Either *"It is well with my soul"* or it's not. There is no middle ground.

Five years ago I had a heart attack. On the way to the hospital, I recall telling my wife not to worry (easy for me to say, not so much for her to hear). I honestly was not concerned about the outcome but fully confident in the sovereignty of God over the affairs of my life. I knew I was going to eventually leave the hospital and journey to one home or the other—either back to my earthly home or on to my other home (preferably to a mansion, of course) in heaven, escorted by angels throwing rose petals at my feet with every step I took. I'm kidding about the rose petals, of course. Besides, I'm not even sure FTD could or would deliver flowers to a heavenly address! In any case, like Paul,

"I'm torn between the two—I don't know which I prefer" (Phil 1:22-24, TPT). I guess I would lean toward sticking around a bit more, though I am at peace with either decision God might make.

I spent the night in the cardiac ICU and woke early the next day before the nursing staff started their morning rounds. As my eyes opened, I greeted the day singing a song written in 1873 by Fanny Crosby. It had been years since I had sung that old hymn. Though she had been blind for most of her life, Crosby saw life clearly (more than most) through the eyes of faith. Amazingly, she wrote more than 8,000 hymns and gospel songs, but none more meaningful to me than the one I sang over and over, ever so quietly and peacefully, as I lay in that hospital bed looking heavenward.

> *Blessed assurance, Jesus is mine!*
> *Oh, what a foretaste of glory divine!*
> *Heir of salvation, purchase of God,*
> *Born of His Spirit, washed in His blood.*
>
> *This is my story, this is my song,*
> *Praising my Savior all the day long…*

There was no reason to be *"anxious"* about anything, *"the Lord is near."* Such faith brings a peace that *"surpasses all comprehension"* for your mind as well as your heart, even while in a prison cell or a hospital ward. (cf. Phil.4:4-7). The apostle Paul knew faith. He lived faith while on a ship that was going down in a stormy sea along the shores of Malta. He experienced faith in a jail at Philippi. He was called to faith along a dusty road to Damascus. Wherever he was, in every circumstance, he believed God: *"that it will turn out exactly as I have been told"* (Acts 27:25). Deep people have deep faith. Corrie Ten Boom, who was sent to a Nazi concentration camp during World War II for assisting Jews, put the key to Christian faith in perspective: *"Never be afraid to trust an unknown future to a known God."*[4]

The "hope of humanity" will not keep you and me unshakable and assured in the midst of sorrow, heartache, and trials. Trusting our future to the conquering, risen Lord of the Ages, Jesus, will! In Him, I can truly *"take heart,"* settle down, and live deeply in a shallow world.

I think I'm going to take the Duke's advice and saddle up anyway!

Endnotes

[1] C. S. Lewis Quotable Quotes. *Goodreads.com,* 2020. https://www.goodreads.com/quotes/615-we-are-not-necessarily-doubting-that-god-will-do-the, accessed September 3, 2020.

[2] Janet Hart Leonard, "A Prayer for Normal and Ordinary Days," *Hamilton County Reporter*, April 11, 2020.

[3] John Wayne Quotable Quotes. *Goodreads.com,* 2020. https://www.goodreads.com/quotes/13533-courage-is-being-scared-to-death-but-saddling-up-anyway, accessed September 3, 2020.

[4] "Beth Harris, "Never Be Afraid to Trust an Unknown Future to a Known God," *MARKALANWILLIAMS.net*, March 26, 2019. Retrieved from https://www.markalanwilliams.net/post/2018/03/15/never-be-afraid-to-trust-an-unknown-future-to-a-known-god.

> *"To forgive is to set the prisoner free and discover that the prisoner was you."*[1]
>
> – Lewis B. Smedes

Chapter 6

Let It Go—Forgiveness

Forgiveness is an essential discipline in the Christian life. Everybody needs forgiveness, and everybody needs to forgive. We've all been hurt or traumatized by what others have done (or have not done) or said. No one can claim innocence in this matter, especially me. Frankly, I've done my fair share of hurtful things as a result of my selfish, self-serving, rebellious behavior and the full use of a rather sharp, destructive tongue. I cannot in good conscience pick up the first stone. I am all out of rocks to throw.

A man I once knew was caught in a police sting designed to grab those soliciting young, underaged prostitutes. He was a highly educated, respected professional in the community. No one suspected his involvement, and his arrest caught everyone by surprise. His behavior hurt a lot of people, which is the way the Devil likes it. The damage was catastrophic, leaving this man emotionally distraught and mentally drained by his own moral failings. His dignity was stripped away, his heart shattered, all remnants of self-respect gone, and his reputation destroyed. So were his career and his marriage. The results of his misdeeds couldn't have been more destructive. In short, he was ruined, and my heart broke for him and his lovely family. I loved that man, and his demise and collapse were hard to watch.

I told my students the heart-wrenching story and asked them if they would consider writing a short note of encouragement to this bruised and bleeding man, expressing their concern for his well-being and offering a little kindness in the process. The goal was to communicate compassion, grace, forgiveness, hope, and redemption at a time when none of it seemed readily available. Many followed through with my suggestion and penned *"beautiful words, wonderful words, wonderful words of life."*[2] The church has sung this hymn for more than 200 years, words of *"faith, hope, and love"* (I Cor. 13:13). I gathered up the notes and sent them off. I received the following response:

> Sandy,
>
> I want to say thank you to you and to your students for the prayer cards. I wept when I read the student comments. Please express my gratitude and repentance to your students for the gift of the cards and prayers. I continue to walk out God's discipline in my life. I daily live in the peace of Christ, regardless of what happens to me in the future. I am thankful for every conversation with you and your wife.

We all need forgiveness (and plenty of it) and a whole lot of mercy tossed in with it. The gospel demands it. Jesus taught it. The apostles lived it. The Scriptures reinforce it, and deep people practice it. Solomon wrote, *"Love prospers when a fault is forgiven"* (Prov. 17:9, NLT). I've witnessed that principle lived out in the life of a little girl.

I was playing for a community soccer club during my first pastorate. I had slowed down quite a bit from my collegiate days and certainly was not the player I once was. But I loved the game and jealously guarded my time and involvement with the local team.

One afternoon I was getting ready to head out the door to soccer practice when my then eight-year-old daughter stopped me and asked if she and her friend could come with me down to the field. My response was none too gracious, to say the least. I snapped, *"This is my time. It's the only thing Daddy gets to do for himself. The answer is no."*

Well, she persisted, and I caved, but with restrictions. I said, "Okay, I'll take you, but you and your friend must stay down on the other end of the field, away from me and the team, and don't bother me until practice is over. Do you understand?" Of course they agreed. So off we went.

As soon as we arrived at the field, I started my training routine. Not ten minutes later (if that), I heard my daughter calling my name as loudly as she could from the other end of the field. *"Sanford! Oh, Sanford!"* She called me by my first name, and that alone irritated me!

I rushed down to the far side of the pitch and scolded them both. I wanted them to know that I was really annoyed. *"What do you want now?"*

You'll never guess.

"We have to go to the bathroom." (I can already see the smile on your face).

God evidently has a sense of humor, though I was not laughing at the time. I obviously couldn't send them off to find a convenient tree or bush. They were girls, so I knew what their pleading meant. I packed them up, got them in the car, and drove them home. I can't tell you how angry and frustrated I was. *"What I feared has come upon me"* (Job 3:25). I just knew something like this was going to happen.

I slammed the car door shut and drove (a little faster than usual) up the hill and back to the house without saying a word. I was fuming on the inside. You could have cut the air with a knife. My daughter, sensing the tension from the back seat, leaned forward and quietly whispered in my ear, *"You know, Daddy, this is nothing to get mad about!"* Though her words were spot on, it didn't help my attitude. In fact, I dug in deeper, determined all the more to make my point and hold on to my self-centeredness and anger. God, however, had other plans. The Spirit knows how to do His job well and bring life-changing conviction.

I pulled hard into the driveway, got out of the car and stomped defiantly up the front stairs and into the house. I was disgusted. *"All right,"* I yelled at the girls, *"go do what you should have done before we left and hurry up about it. I'm not waiting long!"*

The girls ran down the hallway to the bathroom. And then the Lord spoke to my conscience. His words cut deep and penetrated the self-serving soul of a shallow man who should have known better. To this day, I have never forgotten what God whispered in my ear that afternoon. His words still make me uncomfortable. The truth can hurt, and it certainly did.

> Hey! Whose time is this anyway? Yours? Or is it My time? Do I not have the right to interrupt your day whenever I want, however I want, and with whomever I want? This is My time, not yours, and I will use it as I see fit to further my plans, not yours. You owe those little girls an apology. Go make this right.

I bowed my head low and with a contrite heart waited for their return. When they finished with their business, the two little girls came running back down the hall, giggling all the way as if nothing were wrong. I got down on my knees and pulled my daughter in close. I

Let It Go—Forgiveness

looked straight into her eyes and said, "Daddy was wrong, very wrong. I shouldn't have acted like that or said the things I did. I love you. Will you forgive me?"

She replied without hesitation, "Oh, Daddy. I forgave you as soon as you did it."

Out of the mouth of babes. No retribution. No revenge. No rejection. She simply "just let it go," and the matter was settled. I am still learning how to do that—and to live deeper and follow in the footsteps of Christ. Indeed, *"Love prospers when a fault is forgiven"*—a lesson on forgiveness that would be severely tested in the years ahead.

Following the rebuilding of the walls of Jerusalem, the book of the Law of God was brought before the people. Ezra the scribe unfolded the scroll and began to read. As they listened, the people wept (cf. Neh. 8:1-9). They heard the truth about themselves, and it wasn't pretty. They were guilty, convicted of failing to comply with the laws of God in their daily routines. They *"became disobedient"* and rebellious (9:26). They failed to *"listen to the commandments"* of God—a serious mistake with very unpleasant consequences. They *"committed great blasphemies"* (9:18), treating God and the Word of God with contempt and disrespect (discarding divine instructions is always a bad move). They were *"stubborn," "stiff-necked,"* and ungrateful for all that God had done on their behalf over the years (9:16-18, 26-30). Truthfully, the list of grievances sounds much like a running commentary on my own shallow life (probably yours too). Along with the stubborn crowd in Jerusalem, I stand before the judgment of God in great need of forgiveness.

Fortunately, the story does not end there. Despite their rebellious spirit and foolish behavior (and I've exhibited plenty of that), the Lord stood by them (as He does by you and me). He always did and continues to do so today. After all, He is a covenant-keeping God who will never go back on His word, run out on His people, or love them any less for their shortcomings and failings. In Nehemiah 1:5, Nehemiah referred to God in the following ways:

- the LORD (*Yahweh*—"the only One Who has always existed, eternal and unchangeable")
- the *God of heaven* (*Elohim*—"the sovereign Creator of the universe")
- the *great and awesome God* (*El*—"the mighty One, the Almighty").[3]

Only a God like that could put up with the likes of me or Paul the persecutor, Peter the coward, Thomas the doubter, and Jonah the rebel, just to name a few. I could probably plug your name in here, too—right after mine.

Nehemiah described the character of God as *"forgiving,…gracious and compassionate, incredibly patient, with tons of love—[He] didn't dump them"* (Neh. 9:17, MSG) even though they deserved it. *"But in your great mercy you did not abandon them to die in the wilderness"* (Neh. 9:19, NLT). He bore *"with them for many years"* (Neh. 9:30).

And so He has put up with me (and you) as well. He let me off the hook on more occasions than I care to admit and forgave me from the cross, and he continues to do so. And for God's mercy and grace extended to me, a sinner *"saved by grace"* (Eph. 2:8), *"dead to sin, but alive to God"* (6:11), and now set free in Christ to live as God intended, I remain eternally grateful. A forgiven man is a deep man, living out the "crucified life" in his daily relationships. He lives right, loves always, shows mercy at all times, and forgives when necessary.

Conversely, a shallow man refuses all of the above. He demands to see justice served (except maybe in his own life). Retribution is the law by which he lives, and grudges are commonplace against those who have treated him/her with contempt and/or disrespect. One overarching rule dominates the thinking of shallow people who have been wronged or abused by others in some way, shape, or form: "In case God goes soft on you, I won't. I will make sure you get what you deserve for how you've hurt me and treated me." Bitterness is the result of an unforgiving spirit. I know from personal experience.

One summer day I was in the backyard playing soccer with my nine-year-old son. We were having a great time together when suddenly, out of nowhere, anger rose up from within my spirit. It really took me by surprise. For the first time in my life, I realized what I had missed growing up—the love and attention of a father (still haunts me some today). I wanted a dad to spend time with me, teach me how to kick a ball, ride a bike, throw a strike, or swing a bat like I was doing with my son. I wanted a dad who would laugh with me and at me, challenge me, confront me, and cheer for me. I wanted that but didn't get it.

I didn't have a father around in my early years. He deserted my mother after a few short years of marriage and left her with two small children under the age of three, my younger sister and me. One day he just got up and walked out the door. We never saw him or heard from him again. He simply disappeared from our lives. Thirty-five years later the unthinkable happened: my sister found my father. For some reason, she wanted to reconnect, but I really had no interest in doing so. God, however, had other plans. He usually does, and He doesn't normally check in with me first to get my approval on whatever it is He wants to do. He just does it and expects me to go along, whether I like it or not. I've got ideas…if only He would ask.

One evening I was in my study closing up a day's work when the phone rang. My wife had just walked into the room to call me for dinner.

Immediately, I turned toward her and announced, "That's my father." I knew it before I picked up the phone. I answered it. He introduced himself, "I am Arthur, your father." But before he could say much more, I abruptly interrupted him.

> Let's not go any further. I have a few questions for you. Why would a man desert his family and his two small children and make no effort to contact them, not even so much as a postcard or a phone call to find out if his kids had food on their table, shoes on their feet, and a roof over their heads? Tell me why? Why would a man do such a horrible thing? Why would you do that?

I did not mince words. I was angry and wanted him to know it. I demanded an answer.

But I also knew what God expected of me—to forgive that man with no strings attached and let him off the hook for what he had failed to do. Honestly, I didn't want to do it. I couldn't do that, at least not until I got a satisfactory reply. What I later realized was that the questions and the demand for answers were nothing more than a feeble attempt on my part to find a reasonable explanation for his behavior and thereby make it easier for me to do what God required— no longer hold him accountable. The strategy failed miserably.

As he attempted to clarify his actions (I think he was caught off guard by my directness), I found myself becoming angrier and more upset as he talked. It wasn't getting any easier. Here was a man, guilty as charged, showing no real remorse for his past sins, trying to explain away what could not be explained, excuse what was inexcusable, justify what was unjustifiable, and defend what was indefensible. I was unmoved by his words, totally unimpressed as my heart grew harder. Forgiveness was far from my thinking.

Let It Go—Forgiveness

Our conversation ended shortly thereafter, and I was still not at peace. So later that night, I told God (and tried to convince myself) that I had forgiven my father and went to sleep thinking the issue was settled. It wasn't. God has a way of testing our commitments—not that He needed to know the level of my commitment. I was the one who needed to know just where I stood on this matter.

Some months later my father and his wife came to our small town for a visit. I walked into the motel room, sat down, and looked him in the eye for the first time in four decades. He sat across from me with his wife next to him. I began the conversation.

> I want you to know upfront that I am the man I am today because of my mother—not you. You had nothing to do with my successes and achievements or the development of my character. She was the one who invested in me. She taught me right from wrong. She stood by me all these years. She was the one who worked long, hard hours, day after day, year after year, so I could get an education and have some semblance of normality. She put clothes on my back. She fed me. She cried with me, laughed with me, and dreamed with me. I owe her everything. I owe you nothing.

Pretty brutal for a first, face-to-face encounter after so many years. I felt it important for my father to know the role my mother played in my life and how appreciative I was of her efforts. Maybe it was my way of throwing a little salt into the wound. I hoped it stung.

Once I finished giving a brief overview of where life had taken me, it was his turn. I was doing fine with his story until he came to the part about making some sort of a commitment (the details a bit fuzzy) to Christ and going on several mission trips. None of that set well with me. I'm not sure I believed him. In any case, not only was I angry (again) at him, but this time I was also angry at God for potentially letting that man off. I thought as he was speaking,

> I can forgive you, but when you die, you miserable sorry excuse for a man, and you stand before the tribunal of God, you will get what you deserve and burn in Hell for what you've done. There will be no hiding then. No excuses.

That was the ace up my sleeve—the judgment and wrath of God. I was certain that someday God would balance the scales and divine justice would be meted out, especially in this case. The man would finally get what he deserved. Now all that was gone, and it became abundantly clear that I had not forgiven my father as I once thought. To the contrary, like the disciples of old, I wanted to *"call fire down from heaven to destroy"* him (Luke 9:54) and toast him (if I could) right there on the spot in the motel room. I wanted to get even in the worst way. I wanted retribution. I wanted revenge, payback for his misdeeds. I wanted him to get what I believed he had coming to him.

Unfortunately, these are the marks of a shallow man who has not fully let go of the past. I realized I had a great deal of work to do—which I eventually did—and was able to move on with my life.

The boundaries of forgiveness are laid out in a familiar prayer Jesus taught his followers. *"Forgive us our trespasses, as we forgive those who trespass against us."* The *"as we forgive"* is central to the gospel. Forgiveness is the cornerstone of the Christian life. Paul said that those *"chosen of God"* forgive each other *"just as the Lord forgave you"* (Col. 3:12-13). That's how we are called to live and love. Having experienced forgiveness for myself and a release from my past, I am free to extend such forgiveness to others.

Let It Go—Forgiveness

A young Martin Luther, the sixteenth century reformer, once said, *"I lost touch with Christ the Savior and Comforter and made of him the jailer and hangman of my poor soul."*[4] If the apostle Peter had thought the same as Luther, his *"faith"* would have never permitted him to bounce back after denying Christ. He wouldn't have turned to *"strengthen* [His] *brothers"* (Luke 22:32), who by the way were also in need of grace and a whole lot of forgiveness for their own failures. Forgiveness relieves the past, restarts the present, and restores the future. A man cannot pass on to others what he has never known himself, the love and mercy of God.

Deep people are forgiving people. They forgive precisely because they themselves have been forgiven by God, Who has released them from a debt they could not possibly repay (cf. Matt. 8:21-35). I still have a ways to go in the forgiving department.

The psalmist wrote, *"There is forgiveness with* [God]" (Psalm 130:4), and it's a good thing, because it's tough (if not impossible) to find any place else in this world to receive mercy other than at the cross of Christ. *"While they were nailing Jesus to the cross, he prayed over and over, 'Father, forgive them'"* (Luke 23:34, TPT). Deep people pray *"over and over,"* much the same way.

Endnotes

[1] "Forgiven Much But I Can't Forgive," *Hope in the Healing.com* (blog), April 18, 2015, http://www.hopeinthehealing.com/2015/04/18/forgiven-much-but-i-cant-forgive/.

[2] P. P. Bliss, "Wonderful Words of Life" (Nashville: Convention Press, 1991), 261, https://hymnary.org/text/sing_them_over_again_to_me_wonderful.

[3] Nathan J. Stone, *Names of God* (Chicago: Moody, 1944), 12, 19.

[4] Dana Kramer-Rolls, "Martin Luther and Forgiveness: a Question of Christian Ethics," *Episcopal Café*, February 18, 2019, https://www.episcopalcafe.com/martin-luther-and-forgiveness-a-question-of-christian-ethics/.

"The purpose of life is not to be happy. It is to be useful, to be honorable, to be compassionate, to have it make some difference that you have lived and lived well."[1]

– Ralph Waldo Emerson
(19th century American poet and philosopher)

Chapter 7

When Common Isn't Good Enough

Recently I watched the movie *Miracle*,[2] based on the story of one of the finest moments in sports history—the 1980 United States Olympic Hockey Team's winning the gold medal against all odds. I was deeply moved. Uncommon passion, focus, resolve, and effort were on display for the world to see. The "boys" refused to lose. Nothing was going to stop them from doing what no one else thought possible. That night they won more than a medal to hang around their necks: they took home honor, admiration, esteem, and the satisfaction of triumph and achievement. They wanted the best, gave their best, and became the best. Deep people bring that same grit and guts to daily life.

Living Deep in a Shallow World

In one scene their coach, Herb Brooks, challenged his team as he was getting them ready to play against arguably the greatest hockey power in the world at that time—the Russians. He used the word common as he spoke with his team. In the battle that lay before them, *"Common,"* he said, *"wasn't good enough."*[2] They would have to be better than that—outwork, outskate, and outhit their opponent at a level greater than ever before. That's what it takes to win. That's also what it takes to serve the kingdom of God—the best I've got—and in the process get a mean reputation in hell.

The word *common* means "ordinary, usual, and familiar"...average, if you will. Frankly, I don't want any part of sub-performance living. I've had enough of that, thank you. I prefer the words *uncommon, extraordinary, exceptional,* and *remarkable.* They have a much better ring, and those concepts are what's required to see victory and to get the most out of every day. Brooks was right. Common isn't good enough. It never has been. It never will be. Deep people who want to succeed in a shallow world know this.

Just before he died in 2011, Dr. John Stott, an extraordinary Bible scholar and author, gave his assistant some advice about living in this world. He simply said this: "Do the hard thing."[3] There is nothing more uncommon than that.

Unfortunately, what is common is to settle for the ordinary, for mediocrity. Run-of-the-mill seems okay in a superficial world. The slogan *"Be the best that you can be"* is downplayed. Average has become the accepted standard by which we judge our actions and achievements, be it on the athletic field, in our professional careers, in the classroom, or (more importantly) in our spiritual lives, which includes our daily activities and personal relationships with God, our neighbor, friends, and family. The passion and willingness to pay the price to be a successful human being in any arena is in short supply. The "want to" may be there, but the drive to get it done is missing. To be a faithful follower of Christ, a great father or mother, or an extraordinary husband or wife as God intended is no easy task. It is *"the hard thing."*

Some time ago on a merchandise table at an AAU basketball tournament, I saw a T-shirt I wish I would have had when I was coaching. I would have worn it every day to practice to silence the whiners and complainers who thought they didn't have to win the right to be on the field or the court. The shirt had the picture of an empty team bench with the following caption underneath: "If you don't like it, play better!" I loved it. Still do. Couldn't have said it any better than that! Common effort will keep you on the bench. Start doing better! Living better! Being better! "If you don't like it, play better!" I suspect that any man or woman with a degree of self-respect would want life on no other terms.

Deep people are motivated toward excellence for the glory of God and the advancement of His kingdom in this world. Paul wrote to believers in Ephesus, *"I want you to get out there and walk—better yet, run!—on the road God called you to travel. I don't want any of you sitting around on your hands. I don't want anyone strolling off, down some path that goes nowhere"* (Eph. 4:1, MSG). The least I can do is to get off my hands and get on with being the man God wants.

> *It may not be on the mountain height*
> *Or over the stormy sea*
> *It may not be at the battle's front*
> *My Lord will have need of me*
> *But if, by a still, small voice He calls*
> *To paths that I do not know*

Living Deep in a Shallow World

I'll answer, dear Lord, with my hand in thine
I'll go where You want me to go...
I'll be who You want me to be.[4]

I dare not do less.

We live in the age of entitlement, where everybody gets a trophy or a Sunday school pin for just showing up; the pursuit of excellence (the best in me, the best of me, and the best from me) is rarely encouraged anymore. We have grown easily satisfied with less effort and lower achievement. We have become experts at manufacturing excuses for our mediocrity and in the process have degraded human dignity and God-given abilities and opportunity. None of this, however, changes the fact that *"Common isn't good enough."* God is worthy of my finest effort day in and day out.

The lives of deep people stand out because they view each day as holding promise. Supreme Court Justice Oliver Wendell Holmes warned, "Many people die with their music still in them [not interested in that, thank you]...because they are always getting ready to live. Before they know it, time runs out."[4] The graveyard maybe the most expensive real estate in the world because buried within are the treasures and riches of people whose lives never reached their full potential. Nothing is more common than that.

I am convinced that God wants something beyond typical. He wants distinctiveness. *Set apart* is the biblical phrase. *Sanctification* is the theological term. We have narrowed the application of that word—spiritualized it to the point that it has all but lost its practical side in daily life. The concept includes an uncommon God taking hold of common, ordinary men and women, then doing something significant with them and in them—like the Potter taking lumps of clay and pressing, shaping, molding, and remaking them until they are perfectly formed and well suited for service (cf. Jer. 18:4). The product of such divine work is an extraordinary individual (a deep man or woman), designed by Heaven to achieve uncommon results—to be in the place of God's choosing, serving His interests, accomplishing His goals, and living and working in a manner worthy of the name of Jesus (Eph. 4:1). That's a tall order, and I've not always felt up to the task nor spiritually fit to represent God in a world that needs to see *"Christ in you the hope of glory"* (Col.1:27). Nonetheless, I am obligated to go deeper.

A former colleague of mine, who worked for a number of years in student life, expressed disappointment in the manner in which he lived out his daily Christian life (who hasn't). However, he saw some hope for himself in the example of Christ and the events surrounding His life and ministry. He posted the following.

> Sometimes I think that my personal experience is too messed up, or that my life is ultimately not conducive to authentic faith. Then I look at the man Jesus. In his lineage are liars, prostitutes, murderers, adulterers, manipulators, cheats, and cowards without a backbone, and a religious snob, who eventually admitted that he was the "chief of sinners"—just to name a few. Add to this that Jesus' mother is pregnant before the wedding, and not by his soon-to-be-dad. A short time later, the possibility of divorce is seriously considered. When he is born, Jesus' mom gives birth to her son in this nasty hole-in-the-wall place. His first bed is exposed to rodents and the elements. Shortly thereafter his folks are on the run from the authorities. Then his dad seems to disappear from the picture altogether. As an adult, Jesus' siblings think that he is a nut-job

and have in mind to put him away. Jesus is constantly criticized for running around with a salty crowd, which he actually does; and he likes them a lot.

I guess there is hope for the rest of us who are wanting to live deeper in a shallow world.

On one level, the life of Jesus seems pretty ordinary and normal to me. He could have grown up in my neighborhood. His behavior was viewed by many as problematic, and His background was sketchy. His family members were all suspect, His motives questioned, and His career choice misunderstood. He became the leader of a street gang that he recruited himself and then sent out, armed only with a radical gospel to "terrorize" the neighborhood with the intent to take over every aspect of people's personal lives. Look a bit closer, and you will find that the life of Christ was anything but *common*.

Jesus was a tradesman, a laborer, an ordinary man from the streets of Nazareth, but He was so much more… He raised a few dead people along the way and healed a few lepers; the blind received sight; the lame stood to their feet. He fed a large, hungry crowd with two fish and a few loaves of bread, and He healed the brokenhearted, giving them a new sense of hope. That is an uncommon life, anyway you cut it. That is a "Miracle"—one Man living an extraordinary life in a shallow world, taking the gifts, talents, and resources given by God, His heavenly Father, and using them all to the best of His ability to make a difference in the lives of others.

I know a man who has lived an uncommon life, though he is too humble to say so himself. It's just part of his DNA to love and invest in people, see the need, and act quickly and decisively to make things better for all concerned. I am glad to call him "friend" and a fellow worker in the gospel. I marvel at his sensitivity and compassion. He feels deeply for people and cares even more. He is driven to see others succeed as is evident in the lives he's touched. Some years back he sent me a few pages from his personal journal, in which he tells of a man he met on a missions trip to Ruhengeri (Rwanda) and the indigenous people of that area. He drove into the city and…well, I'm going to let him tell you the story—a story about compassion, human dignity, and an uncommon life committed to serving Christ and bringing a little joy to a man who had no name.

> Imagine life without a name. It's hard to, isn't it? That thought, I can honestly say, has never crossed my mind in my lifetime. Is there a thought as sad? Perhaps. I can't think of it though. When a baby arrives in this world, a name is chosen for him/her that they will carry for their lifetime unless they are a musician named Prince who would rather be known as a symbol instead. In the states, we typically select a name before the birth and quickly thereafter send a postcard announcing the arrival of…well, you know. In many tribal cultures, a name is not given for a period of months or years because of the high percentage of infant mortality and deaths due to malnutrition or illness. So in many ways, when a name is given, it is an announcement and recognition of a new and valuable life.
>
> From this point on, one begins to build a reputation, an identity, and a life based on that name. In Proverbs it talks of the value of a good name being greater than riches…or for the "kids" out there…more valuable than 22-inch spinners and a lot of bling-bling on your neck. That is how important and valuable a name can be. So, if I may ask again, what if you had no name?

Living Deep in a Shallow World

Well, I shared a warm bottle of Fanta yesterday with a man with no name. He was unshaven, with unkempt hair, a mouthful of broken teeth tinted in strange fashion, and embraced loosely by ratty clothes. He is both deaf and dumb. Noises with no shape or rhythm pour out of his mouth while his evermoving hands gesture wildly, at war with the air it seems. He is a man easily discarded or shoved to the side. That is one's first reaction to him as he approaches in his crazy manner. You know what though, even though he can neither hear nor speak, there is a way to communicate with that man…through love, time, and sharing…a half a Fanta perhaps.

To be honest, my first instinct as he approached was to step by him with a quick, meaningless handshake and a pat on the back. I was tired from six hours of travel over terrible lava rock roads, exiting from a cramped van with a sliding door that would not close and an inside panel that I had to hold on to because it fell through the bottom of the van earlier and as we pulled out of the small town of Ruhengeri. I was tired from pushing our broken-down van out of the mud and down the road to restart it AGAIN because the battery went George Washington on us…dead. I was tired. I had a long hike up a mountain with darkness quickly falling and my headlamp was not present at roll call for the trip. I ducked in a little clapboard shop for a quick Fanta with a friend from that town. It was dimly lit, attended by a small boy. I paid him and the liquid felt good on my dusty throat.

The man that I conveniently sidestepped on the street had followed us to the shop's door and was being harassed to leave by those outside, and his guttural sounds were met with shoves and words that he could not hear but could feel maybe. I looked him in his eyes…invited him in and handed him what remained of my Fanta. I asked my friend Teogen his name, as Teogen had grown up and lived his entire life there. "He has no name," he simply replied. "How could he anyways? He can't hear it or speak it if he had," he said. "He cannot read so you cannot write to communicate either."

I thought to myself what it would be like to trade lives with that man, for even a day. Slowly, all my hang-ups for the day seemed to fall away. The tiredness, hunger, thirst, thoughts of dark paths up a mountainside, and mainly, my own pride… and I stood there broken inside. Broken for this man, who had never once been called by name. Who didn't know the true beauty of a deep friendship. Who would never know the feeling of being called to and recognized through the privilege of relationship. Who, his entire life, has been in an isolated state of silence, wandering through a world of finger pointers, rock throwers, and those who choose to push him away because of the grunts and moans that spill uncontrolled from his mouth.

It was if mud was removed from my eyes. I no longer saw this man as an outcast from society…I saw him as he should be seen, a man…a man created in the image of God. A man desiring friendship and recognition with a smile instead of a shove. A man on the inside no different from me or any other man.

It was cool to see how the language of love crosses all borders. My lips moving silently met his smile, and his loud cries met my smile, and we just spent time together. Through hands moving less wildly than before, we had a conversation…he made kicking motions and touched his eye to let me know he had seen me play and coach in his village. He formed a beard with his hands to ask about where Elky was as he had seen him a month or so before. I made airplane wings with my hands and made a smooth landing between cups of African tea and a forest of hands…and the conversation continued.

As I began the climb up the mountain in fading light, the village growing smaller and smaller below me, I began to reflect on my new friendship and realized that love resides in the eyes, not the spoken word. Although kind words are good communicators of love, if you want to play a game of hide and seek with love, be sure to check the eyes first.

So do you know a person without a name? I did, once. Not anymore. I never have had the honor of selecting a name for someone before other than the odd pet turtle or lizard, and so you better believe I was jumping on this opportunity with my new friend. I call him Johnny when I see him now…I wanted him to have a cool name, so I gave him the name of one of the coolest cats around I figure…Johnny Depp, although the resemblance is scant at best. He may not hear me yelling, "What's up, Johnny?!" through a crowded market, but when I throw my arm around him and look him in the eye, I think he knows… he finally got a name.[5]

Spurgeon said, "One of the greatest rewards that we ever receive for serving God is the permission to do still more,"[6] touching the lives of people in meaningful and significant ways. That is the focus of a deep man living out an uncommon life in a shallow world, making a difference in the lives of people for the glory of God.

When a lifetime of kingdom work is done at day's end and God calls His own to Himself, the greatest reward of all will be to hear the Master's voice speak your name before all the hosts of Heaven and the saints of glory, *"Well done, my good and faithful servant"* (Matt. 25:21, NLT). They may be the very first words you hear God say to you in Heaven, words that deep people, living uncommon lives, yearn to hear.

Endnotes

[1] Darius Foroux, "The Purpose of Life Is Not Happiness, It's Usefulness," *Observer*, 11/07/16, https://observer.com/2016/11/the-purpose-of-life-is-not-happiness-its-usefulness/.

[2] *Miracle*, directed by Gavin O'Connor (March 20, 2003; Lake Placid: Walt Disney Pictures, February 6, 2004) DVD.

[3] David Brooks, "A Holy Friend," *The Gathering*, Oct. 2, 2014, https://thegathering.com/david-brooks-holy-friend/.

[4] Mary Brown, "I'll Go Where You Want Me to Go," *Timeless Truths Free Online Library* (Public Domain. 1891). Retrieved from https://library.timelesstruths.org/music/Ill_Go_Where_You_Want_Me_to_Go/.

[5] Joey Johnson, "Lifted from My Journal Logged Some Time Ago." Used with permission.

[6] Charles Spurgeon, *AZQuotes.com*, https://www.azquotes.com/author/13978-Charles_Spurgeon, retrieved April 29, 2020.

> "When the whites came to South Africa, they brought the blacks the Word of God and taught them to bow their heads, close their eyes and pray. When they opened their eyes and lifted their heads, the whites got the land, and the blacks got the Book, the Word of God. We shall see who got the better deal!"
> – Desmond Tutu, 1984 Nobel Peace Prize

Chapter 8

A Light Unto My Path

MY JOURNEY, LIKE the journeys of so many others, has had its twists and turns over the years. Better directions and a little guidance along the way wouldn't have hurt. More importantly, a deeper understanding of where I was headed and why I was headed there would have certainly helped me sooner than later get off the *"broad road"* (cf. Matt. 7:13) and away from foolish choices and even worse behavior. I needed a frame of reference (still do), an "instrument" of sorts to keep me level and straight and help me avoid the hazards of "flying by the seat of my pants," which is always dangerous.

I remember from my old Air Force days (teaching aviation physiology) that pilots were taught to trust their instruments first, not their "feelings" or their senses. To do otherwise, particularly in turbulent weather, was to invite disorientation and ultimately disaster.

For deep people, the Word of God is the instrument they've come to trust. They get their reading, establish a heading, and then use it throughout daily life to provide understanding, insight, and much needed help to interpret (make sense of) the world. Bringing direction, order, structure, and meaning to every decision and action taken, the Bible, in short, is the lens through which everything else becomes clear. According to David, God's Word is *"a lamp to my feet and a light to my path"* (Psalm 119:105, AMP). *"By your [God's] words,"* wrote the psalmist, *"I can see where I'm going"* (Psalm 119:105, MSG), and for that very reason, deep people love and revere the Scriptures. They are, after all, the *"words of eternal life"* (John 6:68) found nowhere else other than on the pages of the Bible.

Never will the Word of God lose its power or fail to accomplish its purpose. *"So will My word be which goes forth from My mouth; It will not return to Me empty without accomplishing what I desire, and without succeeding in the matter for which I sent it"* (Isa. 55:11, NASB). That was the promise of Christ (cf Luke 18:31, 24:44. From cover to cover, *"Thy word is truth"* (John 17:17), providing security, stability, confidence, and great courage to face the rigors and trials that often come to an individual. The truth that Jesus spoke of informs the intellect, and the intellect informs the heart for people living deep in a shallow world. Both the mind and the heart are needed and precisely in that order. In short, a deep man or woman is a Christian because Christianity is true. The people of Asia Minor, whose faith had come under attack by those *"denying the Master"* (II Peter 2:1), needed assurance and a reminder to rely solely on the trustworthiness and inerrancy of the Word of God to get them through the ups and downs of daily life.

Feelings are unstable. Personal experience is unreliable. And culture changes with the wind. The only sure word is God's Word, the Bible, where the great issues of life, death, and eternity are defined and on display for all to see. The evidence is in.

Gladys Aylward was convinced that God was calling her to war-torn China. She tried to find the means or some organization that would send her, but she was repeatedly turned down, facing one obstacle or another. No resources. No support. No encouragement. Just rejection and denial, to the point that she questioned her own calling. She didn't have the right qualifications—insufficient education, no knowledge of the language. *"Put the thought of China out of your head,"* she was told. But one night, discouraged and disheartened, she picked up her Bible, and God spoke clearly and decisively. She wrote in her autobiography of that defining moment.

> I pulled out my Bible. "I don't really know enough about this to start preaching to other people," I said to myself as I turned over the pages, "Maybe I ought to set about really getting to know it."...So I started to read...I read on until I came to Abraham. "Now the Lord said to Abram, Get thee out of thy country...unto a land that I will show thee: and I will... make your name great; and thou shall be a blessing (Gen. 12:1-2)."
>
> That verse pulled me up sharply. Here was a man who had left everything—his home, his people, his security—and gone to a strange place because God told him—Maybe God was asking me to do the same."[1]

She thought, *If I want to go to China, I have to be willing to move and give up what little comfort and security I have.* Three days later she picked up her Bible again, and God confirmed her calling to China. She read of Nehemiah who *"wept and mourned"* over Jerusalem, much like she did over China. And the words *"but he did go"* found in the second chapter of that prophetic book caught her attention.

> She shouted, "He went in spite of everything!" then continued reading. "As if someone was in the room, a voice said clearly, 'Gladys Aylward, is Nehemiah's God your God?'"
> "Yes, of course," I replied.
> "Then do what Nehemiah did, and go."
> "But I'm not Nehemiah."
> "No, but assuredly, I am his God."
> That settled everything for me. I believed these were my marching orders.[2]

God's Word eventually took her to China. From the pages of holy writ, God spoke into her life, and a frail but deep woman with no resources of her own and no direction except a word from God eventually led a hundred orphans by herself without food and water through the mountains of China to escape the invading Japanese armies. It was a miracle journey, a demonstration of what the power of God's Word can do in the hands of a deep man or woman. A power that will transform a life and change the world.

> *"And so we have been given the prophetic word—the written message of the prophets, made more reliable and fully validated by the confirming voice of God on the Mount of Transfiguration. And you will continue to do well if you stay focused on it. For this prophetic message is like a piercing light shining in a gloomy place..."* (II Peter 1:19, TPT).

The Bible is the only book ever written that was kissed by the lips of

God—every word "breathed out" from the mouth of Almighty God to say something of vital importance to the world about this life and the life to come.

Donald Cargill, a Presbyterian pastor who committed his life to the teaching and proclamation of the Scriptures, was arrested in Scotland and later martyred in 1681 for *"believing and declaring that Jesus Christ was the true head of his Church."* As he mounted the scaffold, he was fully confident in the inspired, written Word of God. There was nothing he respected or revered more. To the end of his journey, he remained a courageous, faithful servant of God. He did not waver. He did not shrink back. He said, *"The Lord knows I go up this ladder with less fear and anxiety than I ever entered the pulpit to preach."*³ The man lived holding the very Word of God in his hands, and he died having staked his very soul on the veracity and relevancy of the Scriptures. He carried that conviction to the grave. One day in eternity, you may very well find Cargill's name listed among the saints *"of whom the world was not worthy"* (Heb. 11:38, KJV), a man who lived deeply and died bravely, a man like Martin Luther whose *"conscience [was] captive to the Word of God"*—a necessity for deep people.

The apostle Paul reminded young Timothy to *"continue in the things you have learned and become convinced of…the sacred writings which are able to give you the wisdom"* (II Tim. 3:14-15). *"All Scripture,"* wrote Paul to his protégé, *"is inspired by God and is useful to teach us what is true and to make us realize what is wrong in our lives. It corrects us when we are wrong and teaches us to do what is right…"* (II Tim. 3:16-17, NLT). Consequently, a deep man (or woman) not only reads the Bible; the Bible actually reads him. It tells us

Who we are.

Where we've come from.

Living Deep in a Shallow World

Where we are.

Where we're going.

It provides the critical information and inspiration for living deep in a shallow world.

Timothy was responsible for leading the church at Ephesus. He was charged by Paul with the task of teaching the Scriptures without compromise or apology (even if it irritated a few people along the way). He was to stand on the authority of God's Word in matters of faith and practice, whether the people listened or not. Billy Sunday said, *"They tell me I rub the fur the wrong way. No I don't. Let the cat turn around!"*[4] The written Word of God (and nothing else) is the foundation upon which to build a quality life, develop a deep, mature faith, and cultivate a meaningful relationship with God. Apart from the will and Word of God, these assets don't materialize.

On the morning of February 4, 1912, Franz Reichelt, an Austrian tailor, arrived at the Eiffel Tower to test his new parachute. He was informed that he had neither the recommended size for the chute nor the altitude necessary to make the jump successfully, but he ignored the experts. The authorities gave him the correct information—get higher before the jump and increase the area of the chute itself. *"It's too small,"* they said. He did neither and chose to go it alone (just like many of us do). After all, he knew better and he knew more, or so he thought.

Reichelt rejected sound reasoning and reliable evidence. Instead, he opted to do as he pleased (sounds familiar, doesn't it), and his decision proved disastrous. He jumped from the Tower, defying conventional wisdom and scientific data, and it cost him dearly. He died on impact and left a hole six inches deep.[5]

Shallow people do the same, going their own way and living out their personal lives as they see fit while ignoring the wisdom and teaching of the Scriptures. Solomon warned, *"There is a way that seems right to a man, but its end is the way to death"* (Prov. 14:12, ESV).

A young woman who came to see me for counseling was struggling with severe depression. In the course of determining the cause of her feelings and emotional pain, I learned that she was living with another woman's husband, a clear violation of God's design for marriage. Adultery is never healthy, and this case was no exception. I suggested that there was a direct correlation between her life choices and her feelings of distress and depression. I assured her that God's Word had something much better for her life, but some things would have to change. She needed repentance (something she didn't want to hear), a shift in her thinking and ultimately in her behavior. She needed to get out of that toxic relationship—and fast; she needed to start living right as God intended. I suggested a simple solution: *"If you do right (believe and apply God's Word and will to your daily affairs), you will feel right* (cf. Gen. 4:6-7) *about yourself and your personal life."*

Initially, she would have none of it and refused to comply with God's standard of living. She made it abundantly clear in that counseling session that life was going to be lived on her terms, not God's and certainly not mine. She would do as she wanted, and eventually she walked out of my office unchanged. She continued in darkness, a lost soul living a shallow lifestyle that never satisfied her deepest longings. Consequently, she remained in turmoil for years— *"There is no health in [her] bones because of* [her] *sin"* (Psalm 38:3, ESV). I actually pressed her a bit more while she was putting on her coat to leave, at least until she told me I was nuts.

Several years later she contacted me again. It was an unexpected phone call. She said,

God told me to call you and to tell you that you were right the night I came for counseling. You were not crazy. You told me the truth, but I wasn't ready to hear it. I want to thank you for your concern and for the love you showed by challenging me that afternoon with God's Word. I eventually got out of that relationship, and I'm now walking with the Lord, doing better and feeling better about myself and my life.

The Bible knows what it takes to bring order and stability to a chaotic, shallow life.

Make me know Thy ways, O LORD;
Teach me Thy paths.
Lead me in Thy truth and teach me,
For Thou art the God of my salvation (Psalm 25:4-5).

The key to living well is found in God's "ways." And the depth of a man's *"salvation"* (the quality of this life and the life to come) is contingent upon a person's willingness to be taught and guided by God's truth, not his own (or anybody else's for that matter). There is no such thing as "my truth" or "your truth." Those phrases may be popular in today's culture, but it's a myth. All claims cannot be true simultaneously. No two truths can be contradictory (coherence). If this is true, the opposite cannot also be true (the law of non-contradiction). Truth is truth (consistent and congruent with reality), and God has the sole market on truth, preserved in His written Word. Keith Meyer observed,

> When I obey myself [and disallow the Word of God to rule my heart], I end up losing fifteen pounds because I can't eat; I have dark circles under my eyes; I spend hours in emergency rooms taking test after test. Then I talk about it endlessly to my wife,

and I slip an Ambien under my tongue every night to get some sleep. It sounds more like the kind of life Lucifer planned for me: to steal my faith, to kill my body, and to destroy my joy, for the *"thief's purpose is to steal and kill and destroy"* (John 10:10, NLT).[6]

In the movie, *The Lord of the Rings: The Two Towers*, Théoden, king of Rohan, was seated on his throne in the Golden Hall. He is described as one *"whose mind is overthrown,"* having been possessed and controlled by evil. He looked old, feeble, emotionally and spiritually impaired; disengaged from reality, utterly helpless, and no longer able to discern right from wrong. Wormtongue, the very personification of all that is evil and wrong in the world, sat beside the king and whispered in his ear to influence his thoughts and decisions. It was a pitiful sight—the shadow of a once powerful, successful man whose life was ruined, overtaken by ill advice. An all too familiar story of shallow men.

But the tale does not end there, not for Théoden, not for us. Help arrived in the form of a White Wizard, Gandalf, who entered the dark, grim throne room of a spiritually and emotionally enslaved man. The wizard spoke with authority and power—life-giving, life-changing words that challenged and countered the evil that had overtaken the king. A battle ensued, a fight for the very soul and future of the man. In the end, wickedness was cast out, and Théoden was released, set free to live and reign again. A remarkable transformation took place. The character and psyche of the man changed—from darkness to light, from weakness to strength, from death to life, from slave to king. This is what happens to those exposed to the life-giving power of the Word of God.

"Too long you've sat in the shadows," Gandalf said to the king, "Breathe the free air again, my friend…your fingers will remember their own strength better if you grasp your sword."[7] The Word of God is the *"sword of the Spirit"* (Eph. 6:17), and any man or woman who would take hold of it, unsheathe it, and wield it to cut through the decisions and actions encountered in daily life will gain the strength and wisdom necessary to move more easily and live more deeply—*"God's Word, a power in the lives of you who believe"* (I Thess. 2:13, PHILLIPS).

The Crossroad

"Now the LORD said to Abram, 'Go forth from your country... and I will bless you...'" (Genesis 12:1-2).

    I am at a crossroad...
        Again.
    Life seems to be filled with them.
        Choices.
    Moments of decision
        so often accompanied by an anxious spirit,
    Unsettling thoughts
        Disquieted feelings
    Annoying little doubts.
        And fear...always fear.

    Nearly every daily choice
        Big
            Or small
                Forever
    Challenging,
        Confusing,
            Contradictory.

A Light Unto My Path

What shall I do?
  Push or pull?
Which way should I go?
  This way or that?
When do I move?
  Now or later?
Where do I turn?
  Here or there?
Heaven!
  That's where.
To words penned by the hand of God.
  The answers rest with Him.
Within the pages of Holy Writ.
  Always did.
    Always do.
      Always will.
"Heaven and earth will pass away" (Matt. 24:35, ESV)
  But the Word of God will not.
    Not now.
      Not ever.

So,
Weary of guessing.
  Worried about consequences.
    Wondering about tomorrow?
My soul looks up.
  "I LIFT UP MINE EYES… to the
    Maker of heaven" (Psalm 121:1, YLT).
Where else do I dare look

Living Deep in a Shallow World

For
  Counsel,
    Comfort,
      Courage…
But to
  The One
  Who is *"the Beginning and the End"* (Rev. 22:13)?

Amid unexpected chaos.
  Sheer confusion.
    An unsteady course of action.
The stuff of modern life…
  My life.
I find
  The Word of God,
    A Word from God
Remains steadfast and sure.
  Calming,
    Convincing,
      Compelling.
"Lift up your eyes…" (Isa. 40:26, NIV),
  The prophet Isaiah was told
    In no uncertain terms.
First, SEE God!
  "Seated on a throne,
    high and exalted" (Isaiah 6:1, BSB).
Good advice
  For flesh and blood
    Wanting to succeed,

A Light Unto My Path

Wanting to know *"the way, and the truth, and the life"*
   (John 14:6, ESV).

The key to successful, daily living
Like Abram
Was seeing
  Beyond himself,
    Beyond his frailties and capabilities,
      Beyond his doubts and fears,
        Beyond his challenges and circumstances,
      Beyond today.

I need that!
To hear from God.
  To behold
The Majesty,
  Splendor,
Sovereignty of the King—
  To rest in the One
    Who *"ALWAYS leads us in triumph"* (II Cor. 2:14).

The choice is
  Simple,
    Straightforward,
      Sacred.
For every saint down through the ages,
  Wanting answers,
Looking for a word from God.
  Ready

>   To make decisions.
> Prepared
>   To take action.
> There could be but ONE conclusion.
>   The prophet Isaiah made his decision.
>   So did Abram.
>   So did Paul.
>   So must I.
> "Here am I. Send me."
> It is the CROSSROAD
>   each man must face.

"*So Abram went forth as the Lord had spoken to him*" (Genesis 12:4).

- Sandy

Endnotes

[1] Gladys Aylward, *Gladys Aylward, the Little Woman* (Chicago: Moody, 1970), 43.

[2] Aylward, 7.

[3] John Foxe, *The New Foxes Book of Martyrs*, updated by Harold J. Chadwick (Gainesville, Fla.: Bridge-Logos, 2001), 309-311.

[4] D. James Kennedy, *Led by the Carpenter: Finding God's Purpose for Your Life* (Nashville: Thomas Nelson, 1999) 8.

[5] Kevin Ashton, *How to Fly a Horse* (New York: Anchor Books, 2015), 88-89.

[6] Dallas Willard, Keith Mayer, et al, *The Kingdom Life: A Practical Theology of Discipleship and Spiritual Formation*, ed by Alan Andrews (Colorado Springs: Navpress, 2010), 137.

[7] *The Lord of the Rings: The Two Towers*, directed by Peter Jackson (December 2002; New York City: New Line Cinema, 2003), DVD.

> *"Prayer does not mean to simply pour out one's heart. It means to find the way to God and to speak with Him, whether the heart is full or empty. No man can do that by himself. For that he needs Jesus Christ."*[1]
>
> – Dietrich Bonhoeffer

Chapter 9

TALKING THINGS OVER WITH GOD

DEEP PEOPLE KNOW how to talk with God. They get alone with Him at some point every day (usually more than once) to hear from Heaven and get divine input on how to handle daily life. Prayer is practical. It is necessary. It is vital to living successfully in a shallow world. C. H. Spurgeon wrote,

> To pray is as it were to bathe oneself in a cool stream, and so to escape from the heat of earth's summer sun. To pray is to mount on eagle's wings above the clouds and get into the clear heaven where God dwells. To pray is to enter the treasure-house of God and to enrich oneself out of an inexhaustible storehouse. To pray is to grasp heaven in one's arms, to embrace the Deity

within one's soul, and to feel one's body made a temple of the Holy Ghost. Apart from the answer, prayer is in itself a benediction. To pray is to cast off your burdens, it is to tear away your rags, it is to shake off your diseases, it is to be filled with spiritual vigour, it is to reach the highest point of Christian health. God give us to be much in the holy art of arguing with God in prayer.[2]

Philip Yancey wrote a book entitled *Prayer: Does It Make Any Difference?* And that is the question, isn't it? If I'm honest, the practice of prayer is not easy—a common experience among the saints. It is a spiritual discipline that leaves me at times frustrated and confused and quite frankly tired, tired of hearing no for an answer, if I hear anything at all. Sometimes I've left my knees deeply disappointed and often angry at the results of my praying and furious at God Who rejected my petitions for reasons known only to Him. Maybe my frustrations are due to the fact that I am trying to connect with a God so big and so smart that I am unable to fully understand or comprehend what He's doing or where He's going with the things that matter most to me. He just does things differently.

I don't always like God's answers, unless of course I get what I want. I don't like His timing. It seems that I'm always waiting on God to act—to do something, anything. Waiting maybe the toughest of all spiritual disciplines since I don't understand the delays, nor do I always appreciate His decisions. And while I am complaining and whining, let me add that I don't like His methods. They can be downright scary and intimidating.

Alan Redpath, former pastor of Moody Memorial Church in Chicago, agreed.

Talking Things Over with God

It is not that we don't want to pray. It is rather that our experience in prayer often is such that we rise from our knees disappointed and frustrated, feeling that we have wasted our time in repeating meaningless, worn-out phrases which somehow do not mean a great deal to us. When we have finished our praying, we can scarcely bring ourselves to believe that our feeble words have been heard or that they can have made any difference in the things concerning which we have been praying. We've said our prayers, but we haven't prayed.[3]

Frankly, I've sometimes struggled with God's plans, which is nothing new for flesh and blood. At times, I can't seem to find the right words when talking with Him. More often, I end up talking (shouting) *at* God as opposed to talking *with* God There is a huge difference between the two. Consequently, I wonder if prayer is really going to help, questioning if anybody is listening or even cares. Sometimes God's silence seems so cruel and detached from real life situations.

If God hears my prayers, sees my tears, and listens to the cry of my heart as the Scriptures teach, I'm thinking that He just needs to get with the program (my program, of course) and attend to my wishes. After all, I've got ideas. Doesn't God know I've got plans, good plans (at least from my perspective)? I have often remarked to my students and friends that I've submitted an application (nearly daily, it seems) for the job and title "Fourth Member of the Trinity," ready to serve as God's personal counselor at a moment's notice. I've actually believed and behaved as if He needs one, especially one like me. He needs some help, so I'm thinking, and I'm just the guy to step up and volunteer to fill the need. By the way, my approval for that position as the Fourth Member, God's personal helper, is still pending. I have yet to hear from Heaven on that one and probably won't ever. I keep checking ZipRecruiter and my email for notice of a divine appointment, but none has come.

It appears that not many people are completely happy with things as they are. Life often falls short of our expectations, and in our dissatisfaction we are quick to hold God ultimately accountable, but certainly not ourselves or anybody else for that matter—just God. And so we pray, or at least imply that God COULD have or at the very least SHOULD have done something different in our lives, something much more to our liking and benefit, but He has chosen not to act. We reason He could have come up with a better solution. In short, we act as if God screwed up. It is amazing how the finite is so quick to explain the Infinite. Admit it. There are some things beyond our comprehension, and even if God would offer an explanation, which He is not obligated to do, who among us would fully grasp His schemes and plan? Dare I say, no one.

Years ago I attended a Jesus festival held on a farm in Western Pennsylvania. One morning thirty thousand people sat in an open field, listening as a speaker said that God created Adam and Eve and placed them in the garden of Eden, but the pair made some poor decisions in opposition to what God wanted. The results were predictable: disaster— a cataclysmic event for creation and for the personal lives of every man and woman born into this world. The speaker then said, "God was surprised by what Adam and Eve did and soon realized He had a problem on His hands that He didn't know what to do with, and thus He determined that He had made a mistake."

What amazed me that morning were the numerous people in the crowd who mindlessly shook their heads in agreement and approval. I turned to my wife and asked, "Are you listening to this? If I am a non-Christian and you tell me that God makes mistakes and that He is incapable of solving a problem He Himself created, pray tell me, why should I commit my life to a God Who screws up, Who makes mistakes? He might make a mistake and screw up my life! And I don't need Him, or anyone else for that matter, to do that. I am fully capable of making a mess of my life all by myself, thank you!"

Job, who suffered much in this life, complained (much like the rest of us) about his plight and about the hardships he was forced to endure. He demanded answers, and God responded with a few questions of His own:

Who is this that darkens counsel by words without knowledge?...
Where were you when I laid the foundation of the earth?
Tell me, if you have understanding.
Who determined its measurements—surely you know!
Or who stretched the line on it?
On what were its bases sunk, or who laid its cornerstone...
Can you bind the chains of the Pleiades,
Or loose the cords of Orion? (cf. Job 38:1-41).

Vance Havner remarked, "God marks across some of our days, 'Will explain later.' One day of green pastures and still waters is followed by dark valleys and miry swamps, and a thousand 'whys' lie unanswered, tabled for future reference."[4]

We've got questions, and yes, there are some that defy a satisfactory answer this side of Eternity. Understand, however, that if the tragedies, brokenness, pain and hurt in our lives do not somehow fit into a divine, redemptive scheme (whether we understand it or do not see it clearly), then all of that misery is meaningless and serves no purpose whatsoever...and THAT is totally unacceptable for any of us.

At times, I've wanted to change God's mind (what a stupid idea that is). I've stomped, screamed, bargained, cried a river of tears, sat on His lap and pulled on His beard, all in a futile attempt to get Him to jump when I say jump and do what I want Him to do and when I want Him to do it. God doesn't play that silly game. But that is precisely what shallow men and women do.

The apostle Paul asked God three times to remove what he called a *"thorn in the flesh,"* which apparently came directly from the pits of hell. Whatever it was (and we're not sure), at the very least it was an annoying, restrictive *"weakness"* (probably some physical and/or emotional sickness), designed to hammer Paul's pride. God heard his plea but turned him down flat. He had another plan (He usually does), and that was to use every trial (*mistreatments, distresses, persecutions, and difficulties*—II Cor. 12:10) to effectively deal with Paul's ego, keeping him dependent upon God and demonstrating the sufficiency of the power of God in Christ to sustain him before a watching world. Paul prayed earnestly but left the results to God (a good move on Paul's part). He was a man *"well content"* with God's final decision—an attitude toward prayer exhibited by deep people who trust God to best handle the matters that concern them the most. That seems key when talking things over with God and settling your *"heart and mind"* (Phil. 4:7) into His plans.

Unlike Paul, my prayer life reflects shallow thinking; that is, I know better and know more than the omniscient, omnipresent, omnipotent God Who called the vast universe into being, designed it perfectly, hung the moon and stars on nothing, and set it into motion with but a word. He never had to lift a finger to complete creation's mission. He just spoke it into existence. Now imagine the audacity of a finite creature like myself telling a God like that what He can and cannot do (I've done it more often than I care to admit) and then getting angry when I didn't get what I wanted, when I wanted it. To think that God really doesn't know what He's doing and that somehow my plans are an improvement over His and therefore should be implemented without delay or question is the height of arrogance and the epitome of human pride. Such are the thoughts of a shallow man living in a shallow world. It's spiritual lunacy. I would do better (like Job) to *"lay my hand on my mouth"* (Job 40:4), shut up, listen up, and quit trying to figure God out, which is an impossible, fruitless task anyway.

Stan Mooneyham wrote in an editorial in *World Vision* magazine:

> Prayer is not just a list of "gimmes" from a child sitting on the lap of a cosmic Santa Claus. It is communication with the One who is wisdom and love. The cattle on a thousand hills are His, but I come to Him in prayer not so much for a few head of cattle as to be reassured that He is there—and here—and that He cares about what happens to me. His hand is more important than what is in it! God is more than a heavenly pinata from which, if I pound hard enough, goodies will drop out.[5]

No doubt, talking with God is always risky, but it gets results and deep people know it. Heaven responds. Things happen. Doors open. Walls crumble. Kingdoms fall. Lions are denied their lunch. I may not always get what I want (probably a good thing), but I am sure that I will get what God wants, and that is His best for my life (my loved ones included) and His glory.

Above all, Jesus wanted the will of the Father to be done. He already knew it was best—an attitude a deep man or woman might strongly consider adopting in talking with God. Life is meant to play out as God determines if it is to count at all for anything significant. The will and Word of God *"must be fulfilled"* (cf. Luke 22:22, 37). Jesus lived and died, committed to the will of His Father. When he was alone in the Garden of Gethsemane, He knelt down (*"fell upon his face,"* Matt. 26:39, BLB) and prayed that God's redemptive plan, which included His suffering at the cross, would be carried out to its fullest without hesitation in His own life and ministry, *"as it has been determined"* (Luke 22:22, ESV), no matter what the cost. It was the *"cup"* Jesus was willing to drink. Living deep demands it.

Unfortunately, I've been more like Jonah, who tried to flee from God and His plans and needed a bit of divine "encouragement" (the board of education applied to the seat of understanding, as they say) to get with God's program. History is filled with examples of men and women who knew how to talk things over with God, align their lives with the heart of God, and walk away with the results they were seeking and needed.

George Mueller (1805-1898) knew how to pray. He built a number of orphanages solely on the faithfulness of God to supply the needs of more than 10,000 orphan children. Adoniram Judson (1788-1850) was a man who spent hours each day talking with God. The power and wisdom he received from those special meetings enabled him to translate the Bible into Burmese and bring thousands to Christ. Miriam, sister of Aaron and Moses, knew how to pray. After the crossing of the Red Sea, she took her tambourine and sang a prayer of celebration of God's victory over Egypt. Hannah knew how to pray, begging God in her heart for a son, and Samuel was born out of her *"distress"* (cf. I Sam. 1:9-20). David was a man of prayer (cf. Psalm 109:4). In fact, he said of himself, *"I am* [in] *prayer."*

Jonah also prayed—after he had a "come-to-Jesus" meeting in the belly of a great fish (a really big one), where He and God got to talking things over (always a smart move when drowning in fish chum and seaweed). God heard his cry for help (cf. Jonah 2:2), rescued the wayward prophet, and gave him another opportunity (that's grace) to declare the mercy of God to a pagan city. Three days later, the fish spit Jonah up on shore. His skin was probably bleached white from flailing about in the guts (stomach acid) of a great fish. He must have been quite a sight, dragging himself out of the surf and onto the beach, but this time he was ready to move forward (a bit reluctantly) with God's mission. God did not change His mind about what He wanted from Jonah, and Jonah never got what he wanted, the judgment and wrath of God to fall on the city of Nineveh and its inhabitants. What God wanted (and got) was for Jonah's life and ministry to be a conduit of the mercy and grace of Yahweh. That was God's plan and purpose, and those living deep in a shallow world eventually want what God desires—first, last, and always.

Nehemiah fasted and prayed *"before the God of heaven"* (Neh. 1:4), looking toward heaven for the go-ahead and the resources to rebuild the walls of Jerusalem, which desperately needed repair (cf. Neh. 1:11). His talk with God paid off. He got what he needed—brick, mortar, and a few masons who also knew how to swing a sword as well as a trowel. Job complete; prayer works.

Moses prayed, and God let loose the plagues on Egypt to force a hard-hearted Pharaoh to release the Hebrew slaves. Joshua talked battle strategy with the *"captain of the host of* Lord*"* and fell on his face, awaiting directions to take the city of Jericho. *"What has my lord to say to his servant?"* (Josh. 5:14). Now that's the prayer of a deep man, who recognizes God's sovereignty, authority, and power over the affairs of men.

Elijah climbed Mt. Carmel to confront the prophets of Baal, did some trash talking while he was up there, threw twelve buckets of water on some wood, and then checked in with God. *"*Lord*…I have done all* *these things at Thy word. Answer me..."* and fire fell from heaven and consumed the sacrifice on the altar. Now that's a prayer!

Manasseh was rotting in an Assyrian jail because he had done more evil (sexual perversion and child sacrifice) in Jerusalem than the pagan nations that surrounded him. His behavior was deplorable, unbecoming a man entrusted with the task of leading the people of God. In the end, Manasseh was captured, dragged off in chains, and locked away in a maximum-security prison run by pagans. He begged God for forgiveness and mercy. God saw his heart and restored him to his throne. Nothing happens apart from passionate, deep prayer. Jonathan Edwards said, "[Prayer] *is an excellent means of keeping up an acquaintance with God,"*[6] a necessary routine for people wanting to live deep. Keep God close at all times!

And then there was Peter, who was put in prison, locked up and under guard by four squads of Roman soldiers. There was no way out. His future looked grim. His death was imminent. King Herod already *"had James the brother of John put to death with a sword"* (Acts 12:1-2) and was out looking for more blood. *"But prayer for him [Peter] was being made fervently by the church"* (Acts 12:5). God was more than a mere "acquaintance" to these early believers. He was real. He was accessible. He was approachable.

"But prayer" are the two words in that story that makes the difference in every situation and circumstance of life. They can change the outcome of eternity. They are powerful, comforting words in an unpredictable, volatile, shallow world. Peter was hopelessly locked in a dark, gloomy prison, *"but prayer"* ascended before God like smoke from the altar (cf. Rev. 8:4). Peter was awaiting execution and the end of his earthly life, *"but prayer"* kept coming *"day and night,"* passionate, intense, persistent praying. The disciples wore out the carpet by the

side of their beds (cf Luke 18:1-8). They would not leave God alone until they had prayed through the matter and got an answer one way or the other. If the king had his way, Peter would not have survived another night, *"but prayer"* was being sent up to God's throne room where the petitions of the saints are carefully weighed out and divine decisions are made in their best interest. Amidst all of this gloom and doom, Peter slept peacefully, resting comfortably between two Roman guards, apparently unconcerned about what tomorrow might bring. Talking things over with God, confident that He will respond in a manner that suits His plans and purpose (not theirs, yours or mine) is the way of deep people.

Frankly, there is no other choice but to pray, especially when we feel cornered and up against trials and tribulations. And isn't that the way it is? Our best praying finds expression in the toughest of days. Oswald Chambers observed, "We do not pray at all until we are at our wits' end."[7]

When a small band of believers gathered at *"the house of Mary, the mother of John"* (v. 12) to fight it out with the powers of hell, they must have felt the same way, *"at wits' end,"* distressed, and worried. But they knelt together before almighty God, the only One they knew who could get Peter out of a jam, rescue him from certain death, and return him to his family, his friends, and his ministry. So they boldly petitioned heaven for his life. They needed God's help and asked for it. They needed a miracle, a supernatural intervention (who doesn't?)… and they got it. David wrote, *"I am passionately in love with God because he listens to me. He hears my prayers and answers them"* (Psalm 116:1-2, TPT). And God did just that (still does).

An angel sent by God entered Peter's cell and poked him in the ribs. *"Get up, son!"* he said. *"We're leaving, right now!"* Peter did what he was told (a pretty good idea when God is speaking to you). He sat up, put on his Nike sandals, stood to his feet, and followed the angel out of the prison—down the streets and alleyways to the iron gate of the city, which Luke reports *"opened by itself"* (cf. v. 10). Sort of reminds me of the automatic doors at Walmart. Peter headed straight to Mary's house. Rhoda, *"a servant-girl,"* heard the knock at the door and came to see who it was. She instantly recognized Peter. Excited and surprised by his presence, she quickly ran to tell the others who were still in their Wednesday night prayer meeting, which I suspect was a bit more explosive and intense than most of us have experienced in the modern church. At first, the group didn't believe her. She pressed them further, and when they checked, they found the man they had been praying for waiting at the front door. Luke records that they were "amazed" (v. 16), astounded to see Peter. They did not expect to get the results they wanted, at least not so quickly. Sounds familiar, doesn't it? Apparently, *"asking, seeking, and knocking always works with God."*[8]

Answered prayer produces both exhilaration and shock. I have been stunned in the past by the demonstration of God's power and goodness. I shouldn't be surprised, but I am. The psalmist invites us to *"Taste and see that the LORD is good"* (Ps. 34:8, NLT), but like Rhoda and the disciples, most of us need some work praying in full confidence that God will always answer our petitions with our best interest in mind and meet our needs (known and unknown), sometimes doing so in ways we never could have imagined. Being stunned when God answers is the plight of a shallow man who prays with reservation when he talks with God, if he talks with God at all.

At times I've lost trust in the sovereignty and love of God, subsequently degrading my belief in the very existence and character of God. Now that's a problem—*"Because anyone who wants to approach*

Talking Things Over with God

God must believe both that he exists and that he cares enough to respond to those who seek him" (Heb. 11:6, MSG). But God does exist and He does care: those two simple, yet profound truths motivate deep men and women to pray *"fervently,"* petition God with the right motives and a solid faith that expects results, and not to *"lose heart"* (Luke 18:1) in the process, no matter what. There is no quitting in prayer for deep people, just a stubborn refusal to give up on God. They stay on their knees (*"without ceasing"*—I Thess. 5:16) for however long it takes.

I can recall the day I prayed—no, really prayed—maybe the most ruthlessly honest prayer I've ever uttered. A family member, suffering from severe depression caused by childhood abuse at a church preschool, showed up at my office one afternoon. She was desperately in need of help, having made several attempts at suicide. She stood in my office and wept, *"I want to live. I really want to live, but God has got to help me. I can't do this on my own."* My heart broke for the young woman, and I arranged to take her for counseling later that day. When she left my office, I did the only thing I knew to do: I prayed. I asked God to intervene, to take control of the situation, and to protect this girl's life. I was helpless, and I knew it. I lacked the strength and wisdom to fix this. I needed God and God alone to step in. So I lifted my tear-filled eyes toward the heavens and asked, *"What kind of a God are You that You can hear such a plea and turn a deaf ear?"* I got my answer, and I got it quickly.

My mind immediately filled with the image of a great throne, and seated thereon was the figure of a man, a King Whose face I could not make out. He rose to His feet, donned His armor, mounted a majestic white stallion, and unsheathed His sword. Behind Him was a vast army as far as my eyes could see and whose numbers I could not count— each one clothed in battle array, ready for a fight, warriors each one, fierce and waiting for the command to go. It was a massive, terrifying display of unmatched grandeur and unimaginable power.

An hour later, I drove the young lady to see a Christian counselor we both hoped would be able to help her. When we arrived, the man handed me a folder, and across the top were scrolled the words "Battle Strategies." I wept when I read it. The man had no idea what I had just witnessed in my mind's eye. He turned toward me and said, "Here. You pray what's in this folder while I fight!" A shallow, weak man was about to learn what it means to fight on his knees. It's how deep people do battle.

Here are some suggestions you might consider when talking to God about those things that matter most to you.

- Make a conscious, deliberate, and willful decision upfront, before you have said one word to God, to trust His goodness and wisdom without reservation.

- Learn to live with ambiguity (*"riddle"*—I Cor. 13:12), with some degree of uncertainty because you don't know (nobody does) what, where, when, why, or how God will respond—nor do you fully understand how He thinks, how He will act, or how He will move, only that He does and He will.

- Be patient; wait on God. Do not give Him a time limit in which to work or expect him to move sooner than He may desire. Remember: "It ain't over till it's over."[9]

- Focus on current and past blessings, encouraging yourself by reviewing/listing all that God has already done in your life. *"Count your blessings, name them one by one."* Do what David did when his wives were taken and the city of Ziklag was burned to the ground—*"David strengthened himself in the* LORD *his God"* (I Sam. 30:6).

- Think long-term about the "results" to be gained, knowing that God has an ultimate purpose that you may or may not immediately see.

- Acknowledge God's lordship and His right to rule over your life by offering yourself to Him anew in whatever situation you find yourself.

- Stop asking "Why?" It serves no real purpose. Refocus your thoughts on the character of God and then rejoice in the Lord because *"the Lord is near"* (Phil. 4:4).

- *"Bless the* LORD, *O my soul, and all that is within me"* (Psalm 103:1). Make a conscious decision not to murmur against God. Instead, decide to speak well of Him to yourself and to the world.

Bronwyn Lea described herself as *"the very biggest fan of Jesus, great healthy relationships, and belly laughter."* She made a suggestion about talking with God amid life's awful tragedies, difficult days, and sometimes unrelenting pain and sorrow—especially when we're not sure of God and where He is taking us. It is a prayer to help us go deeper with Him and stay centered on eternity and God's kingdom. She wrote,

> Instead of praying "God, make it better," I need to pray, "God, make it count."
>
> "God, my friend is dying. Don't just make it better, make it count. If she can be better, let it be so, but don't let this suffering have been wasted. Work it for good. Please show up and show your grace. Make it count."

"God, I'm so busy and so tired. I so badly want to pray 'Make it better! Make it stop!' but I'm going to pray, 'Make it count, please' instead. Let me learn grace under fire....Show your strength in my weakness."[10]

Deep people make it count when talking with God.

THE OTHER MAN

"Now there is in Jerusalem by the sheep gate a pool, which is called in Hebrew Bethesda, having five porticoes. In these lay a multitude of those who were sick, blind, lame, and withered. ...A man was there who had been ill for thirty-eight years. When Jesus saw HIM...He said to him, 'Do you wish to get well?'" (John 5:2-6).

I am the other man, like so many.
   Disfigured
      Defective
         Detestable in the eyes of some;
A dreadful, *"withered"* man.
   A soul scarred by hopelessness
      A heart sick with disappointment
      A spirit lame and motionless
         A mind blinded by doubts.

I am the other man
   At the Pool *"called Bethesda"* (v. 2),
      The man Jesus looked past,
   Stepped over,
   Walked by.

Talking Things Over with God

One of *"a multitude"*
  Desperate,
    Disillusioned,
      Demanding!
God's attention.
  God's power.
    God's compassion.
I need healing, too.
  A miracle.
    A change.
      A future.
So
I hope.
Beg.
Pray to God,
  "Look at ME.
    Take ME.
      Heal ME!"
Make the pain stop!
I DO want *"to get well!"*
I want…
  A brighter day,
    Joy in the morning!
      A sweet song to sing.

Surprisingly,
  An answer comes,
  But not for me;
A divine command is issued,

> But not for me;
> *"Arise…walk!"*
>> And *"immediately"* healing came to a broken man
>> (John 5:8-9).
> Supernaturally,
> God did what only God can do,
>> But not for me.
> Sometimes it seems my plea goes
>> Unrecognized,
>>> Unnoticed,
>>>> Unheeded.

> Accordingly,
> Heaven's silence is
>> Deafening
>>> Disrupting
>>>> Disturbing.
> One man is raised,
>> One man remains.
> One man walks away,
>> One man remains.
> One man is made whole,
>> One man remains.
> **I am that other man…**
> Pounding on heaven's gates
> Wanting answers
> "Why him,
>> and not me?"
> Nothing seems to make sense.

Talking Things Over with God

For a brief, torturous moment,
I surrender to self-pity.
  Incensed,
    Infuriated,
      Whining about lost opportunities.
Tomorrow seems
  Uncertain
    Undefined
      Unfinished.
Fearful of what may never be.
Jealousy haunts me.
  Shameful envy.
    Bitter disappointment.
Wanting,
  No, demanding
What God is pleased to do for another,
  But not for ME.
Lamenting over this simple, yet destructive possibility;
Just maybe…
God is
  Displeased with me,
    Dissatisfied with me,
      Disappointed in me.

NO!
  A THOUSAND TIMES, NO!
Stop this insanity!
  "Bless the LORD, O my soul;
    And all that is within me…FORGET none of His benefits…"

God is NOT mad at me.
The cross screams otherwise.
For there reconciliation was
   Secured,
      Sealed,
         Safeguarded…forever.
Finally,
Peace with God.
   Peace from God,
      And the peace of God to enliven a saddened heart.
There *"At the cross,*
   where I first saw the light,
      the burden of my heart rolled away."[10]
Divine love was poured out.
   Unmeasured.
      Overflowing,
         Encircling.
A new day is coming.
A new dawn.

The Son is rising through the darkness,
And a tomb is left empty.
   Resurrection power is unleashed
To lift a "downtrodden" man;
A *"captive…set free"* (Luke 4:18).
   Relieved
      Restored
         Revived.
Good news!

My life redeemed *"from the pit"* (Psalm 103:1-4),
Like Joseph.
Now
   Empowered,
      Energized,
         Encouraged.
I CAN LIVE BEING THE OTHER MAN.
Come what may…
   "Content in whatever circumstances
      I am" (Philippians 4:11)
To serve the purpose of God.
   Satisfied.
      Grateful.
         Complete…
I'm okay.

   - Sandy

Endnotes

[1] Dietrich Bonhoeffer, *Psalms: The Prayer Book of the Bible* (Minneapolis: Augsburg Fortress, 1970), 9-10.

[2] C. H. Spurgeon, *Effective Prayer* (Pensacola: Chapel Library, 2015) 162-165, Kindle.

[3] Alan Redpath, *Victorious Praying* (Chicago: Fleming H. Revell Company, 1957), 12.

[4] Allen Webster, "When Life Doesn't Make Sense," *House to House Heart to Heart*, https://housetohouse.com/when-life-doesnt-make-sense/.

[5] Stan Mooneyham, Editorial, *World Vision*, Dec. 1980, 23.

[6] Peter Beck, "Jonathan Edwards and Prayer," *Church and Gospel*, Feb. 12, 2016, http://www.churchandgospel.com/2016/02/12/jonathan-edwards-and-prayer/.

[7] Oswald Chambers, *Our Ultimate Refuge* (Grand Rapids: Our Daily Bread, 2006).

[8] John Nolland, *The New International Greek Testament Commentary: The Gospel of Matthew* (Grand Rapids: Eerdmans, 2005), 7:8.

[9] "Yogi Berra Quotes," *BrainyQuote.com*, BrainyMedia Inc, 2020. https://www.brainyquote.com/quotes/yogi_berra_110034.

[10] Bronwyn Lea, "One little word that radically changed my prayers," *Best of the Blog*, 2019. https://bronlea.com/2013/08/06/one-little-word-that-radically-changed-my-prayers/.

> *"There is no authority powerful enough to force your life to yield to God the Holy Spirit who alone can give you victory, blessing, power, and usefulness. The tragedy unfolding year after year in the life of some Christians is that they remain on the shelf as far as availability to God is concerned."*[1]
> – Alan Redpath

Chapter 10

A Living and Holy Sacrifice

I owe God (so do you)…everything. Consequently, I'm not interested in living life "on the shelf," unavailable and indifferent toward serving the kingdom of God in the place of His choosing. It's as simple as that. Everything I am or will become, everything I have, every person I've ever rubbed shoulders with (troublesome or otherwise), every recognition I've ever obtained, every position I've held, every slice of pizza (and especially cheesecake) that's ever passed my lips, every strand of hair (or lack thereof) on my head, every breathe I take, every step I make, even the glasses I wear and the clothes on my back are the product of the goodwill and good graces of God. In Christ, *"all things hold together,"* and that includes my life and yours as well. Surrender, service, and sacrifice for the cause of Christ and the advancement of His kingdom in my little corner of the world are not only appropriate but necessary and, I dare say, divinely expected.

Paul addressed the intellectuals of his day (the ones supposedly with all the brains) who apparently missed a small but very important fact when thinking of the great issues of life, death, and eternity—that *"in Him* [Christ] *we live and move and exist"* (Acts 17:28). For that reason, Christ must *"come to have first place in everything"* (Col. 1:17-18). The Greek adjective translated *everything* means (wait for it)… "everything"—"total, all, the whole enchilada." No exclusions. The demand of Christianity is clear. Actions must follow beliefs. Word and deed are intricately connected, and that is exactly the case with men and women who are living deep in a shallow world, who freely lay their lives down on the altar each day (everything they are and everything they have), bound to God by cords of faith and love, much like young Isaac on Mt. Moriah.

On that mount, Abraham and his son sacrificed their wills and their very lives for the sake of obeying God in holy living and service to His kingdom. Authentic faith in Christ expects sacrifice, no demands it—*"He must increase and I must decrease"* (John 3:30). The words of John the Baptist apply to every facet of the believer's daily life. Nothing held back. *"So here's what I want you to do,"* wrote the apostle Paul to the Christians at Rome, *"God helping you: Take your everyday, ordinary life—your sleeping, eating, going-to-work, and walking-around life—and place it before God as an offering"* (Romans 12:1-2, MSG).

Ravi Zacharias died (May 2020) after serving Christ for many years as a distinguished apologist and evangelist, traveling the world to engage and challenge his generation with the truths of the gospel. Several months prior to his death, he received the troubling news—cancer. His family remembered his reciting the words of an old church hymn soon afterward. The words were written by Richard Baxter in 1681.

> *Lord, it belongs not to my care*
> *Whether I die or live:*
> *To love and serve Thee is my share,*
> *And this Thy grace must give.*
>
> *If life be long, I will be glad,*
> *That I may long obey;*
> *If short, yet why should I be sad*
> *To welcome endless day?*
>
> *Christ leads me through no darker rooms*
> *Than He went through before;*
> *He that unto God's kingdom comes*
> *Must enter by this door.*
>
> *Come, Lord, when grace hath made me meet*
> *Thy blessed face to see;*
> *For if Thy work on earth be sweet*
> *What will thy glory be!*
>
> *Then I shall end my sad complaints*
> *And weary sinful days,*
> *And join with the triumphant saints*
> *That sing my Savior's praise.*
>
> *My knowledge of that life is small,*
> *The eye of faith is dim;*
> *But 'tis enough that Christ knows all,*
> *And I shall be with Him.*[2]

Deep words from a deep man whose life had become a living sacrifice to the glory of God.

His daughter Sarah wrote of her father:

> He turned every conversation to Jesus and what the Lord had done. He perpetually marveled that God took a seventeen-year-old skeptic, defeated in hopelessness and unbelief, and called him into a life of glorious hope and belief in the truth of Scripture—a message he would carry across the globe for 48 years.[3]

His was an incredible legacy of faith and sacrificial service.

During World War II in 1939, Dietrich Bonhoeffer struggled with the decision whether to return to Nazi Germany or to remain in the shelter of the United States. He was torn between his own safety and his deep commitment to confront and challenge the German church, which was slowly but surely caving to Hitler's demands and adopting the doctrines of the Third Reich. No longer did the church stand without compromise or apology for God's authoritative Word. It had strayed far from solid, practical, biblical theology and lost its influence for good within the borders of the nation. Bonhoeffer was driven to see the German church change and recapture its faith, once again showing forth *"the light that shines in the darkness"* (John 1:5). He knew the risks. He knew the threats—imprisonment and execution, but he returned anyway under the compulsion of the Spirit of God, ready to make whatever sacrifice was necessary to fulfill his divine calling. He went back to Germany to serve the kingdom of God as a prophet who "would share in the sufferings of Christ."[4] Some years earlier, Bonhoeffer described a change that had taken place, feeding his restlessness and giving him a clear vision of the call of God upon his life.

> Then something happened, something that has changed and transformed my life to the present day. For the first time I discovered the Bible...I had often preached. I had seen a great deal of the Church, and talked and preached about it—but I had not yet become a Christian...I was quite pleased with myself. Then the Bible, and in particular the Sermon on the Mount, freed me from that. Since then everything has changed. It was a great liberation. It became clear to me that the life of a servant of Jesus Christ must belong to the Church, and step by step it became plainer to me how far that must go. The revival of the Church and of the ministry became my supreme concern...My calling is quite clear to me. What God will make of it I do not know...I must follow the path."[5]

Bonhoeffer had a choice: life on Hitler's terms or life on God's terms. The latter meant death to self. He chose the gallows rather than forsake his faith and in so doing became a *"living sacrifice,"* a man who refused to accept "cheap grace" in himself or in the teaching of the church. He was hung by the Nazis for treason one week before the end of the war. *"He who believes in Me,"* Jesus said, *"shall live even if he dies"* (John 11:25). Certainly from a human perspective, it would appear that Bonhoeffer chose death, but not so. He embraced life, a deep life, as a follower of Christ—*"by loving the Lord your God, by obeying His voice, and by holding fast to Him"* (Deut. 30:19-20), regardless of personal cost. To live for Christ till the very end and so bear the scars of Calvary upon his heart and life was his lot.

Herein are the marks of a deep man, holding nothing back in this world and producing *"much fruit"* by the manner in which he lives and dies (cf. John 12:24). His influence extended to the next generation and beyond. "The reward for service," said D. L. Moody, "is more service"[6]—that is, a life focused on generating significant results in kingdom work and achieving lasting, positive outcomes for the cause of Christ.

A widow with only a few pennies to her name also made an incredible, selfless sacrifice at the temple treasury in Jerusalem. She gave till there was no more to give. She sacrificed everything, and it caught Christ's attention. From among the *"multitude"* that had gathered that day, Jesus singled her out and set her before the disciples as a prime example of deep living, genuine faith, and a commitment to God few know.

> *And He looked up and saw the rich putting their gifts into the treasury. And He saw a poor widow putting in two small copper coins. And He said, "Truly I say to you, this poor widow put in more than all of them; for they all out of their surplus put into the offering; but she out of her poverty put in all that she had to live on"* (Luke 21:1–4).

That last phrase, she *"put in all that she had to live on,"* penetrates to the core of my soul, like a sharp, two-edged sword. It cuts deep. His words challenge, convict, and certainly cause me to feel most uncomfortable. *"All that she had"* hurts because it takes me well beyond mere church attendance, singing a few hymns, and tossing God a few bucks when the offering plate passes. She didn't give much, because by the world's standards she didn't have much. But she gave it anyway. Every last possession of any value and importance to her well-being and daily life was surrendered to God for His use. Nothing about this sacrifice was cheap. From the very start, it wasn't about the money. It never was, and it never is. This story is about her most prized possession—her heart. That is what she brought to the temple that day, and that is what Jesus saw.

A Living and Holy Sacrifice

Nothing is of greater value than my heart; God wants it more than anything else. He died for me and thus owns the right to possess my heart—all of it. Nothing less will do. When I compare my own response to God's claim upon my life, I am left with a dwarfed view of myself in the presence of this remarkable woman. Two thousand years later her actions of faith and commitment still haunt me, and they should you, too.

God demands all of me, the deepest part of me, and He will hold out until He gets it—the whole of my life. The words of Cardinal John Newman from the nineteenth century are pasted in the front cover of my Bible. I carry them everywhere as a reminder. "If I am in sickness, my sickness may serve Him; in perplexity, my perplexity may serve Him; if I am in sorrow, my sorrow may serve Him."[7] That about covers everything—both the good and the bad laid at the feet of the Savior.

No doubt, when I consider the cross and what it cost God for my redemption, I owe Him big time. After all, I am not my own. Never have been. I have been *"bought with a price"* (I Cor 6:20). It's just that simple. I owe him my life—my ambitions, my hopes, my dreams, my achievements, my awards, my time, my talents, and my treasure. I owe Him this day and every hour of every day for that matter. I owe Him the clothes on my back and the food on my table, as well as my home, my cars, my health, my future, my marriage, my children, my tears, my laughter, my loneliness, my disappointments, my brokenness, and my deepest hurts. As a pastor or as a church leader, I owe God my study, my sermons, my pulpit, and ultimately, the church I serve. It was never mine anyway. No holdouts.

In short, I owe God my all (however much or little I have) to be used by Him for the advancement of His kingdom in whatever capacity He sees fit and for however long He needs and wants me and my "stuff." But most of all, I owe Him my heart, for out of the *"abundance of the heart"* flows every decision I make and every action I take. If He owns my heart, He owns everything else. Behavior always expresses what the heart truly values.

There is no question what that woman outside the temple treasury valued in life. She *"put in all that she had to live on."* Obviously, she thought more highly of God than her own comfort, security, and life itself. How reckless, even irresponsible some might say. To the average, shallow onlooker, her sacrifice may have looked foolish and shortsighted.

But that's how faith looks sometimes, a bit wild—and I could use a little more of that in my own personal life and ministry. The woman had the audacity and daring to trust God with the details of her life, not fully knowing what tomorrow or even the rest of her day might look like. Who would do such a thing? I suspect she had no idea where her next meal was coming from or how she would take care of herself the next day, and the next, and the day after that. She had but one thing on her mind and heart—God alone was worthy of her very best. He is worthy of my very best. Nothing less. He deserves more than my leftovers.

The amount (two small coins) the poor woman offered to God wasn't what drew Jesus to her. It was how much she had left over. And that amounted to ZERO. She held nothing back. Exhausted and drained, she opened her heart first and then her purse, presenting to God whatever she had at her disposal until all her personal and physical resources were depleted. She spent herself for the kingdom of God. Her story is my story and yours (at least it should be).

So I have to ask, "What do you really value?" If indeed you are living deep in a shallow, self-serving, self-promoting world, the answer to that question will reveal your true heart. Let's take up an offering! Surrender your best. Be a living sacrifice.

Endnotes

[1] Alan Redpath, The Making of a Man of God, (London: Pickering & Inglis LTD, 1962), 14.

[2] Richard Baxter, "Lord, It Belongs Not to My Care," *Timeless Truths: Free Online Library*, 1681, https://library.timelesstruths.org/music/Lord_It_Belongs_Not_to_My_Care/.

[3] Sarah Davis, "Ravi Zacharias, Now with Jesus," RZIM, May 2020, https://www.rzim.org/read/rzim-updates/ravi-zacharias.

[4] Eric Metaxas, *Bonhoeffer: Pastor, Martyr, Prophet, Spy* (Nashville: Thomas Nelson, 2010), 123-24.

[5] Metaxas, *Bonhoeffer*.

[6] William R. Moody, *The Life of Dwight L. Moody* (New York: Fleming H. Revell Company, 1900), 319.

[7] John Henry Newman, *Meditations and Devotions of the Late Cardinal Newman* (London: Longmans, Green, and Co., 1893), 301.

> "*We do not want, as the newspapers say, a church that will move with the world. We want a church that will move the world.*"[1]
> —G. K. Chesterton

Chapter 11

TURN THE WORLD RIGHT SIDE UP!

DEEP MEN AND women are forever getting themselves into trouble with the world. Challenge secular values, criticize cultural behaviors, or confront popular thinking, then have the audacity to offer a biblical alternative (which has always been standard operating procedures for Christians), and you are going to upset a few people. It's going to happen. Expect it. The gospel is truly the *"disruptive force of revelation,"* and as believers we are called *"to speak the gospel in a way that unsettles the listeners,* [and] *conveys the transcendence of God..."*[2]

Paul and Silas were beaten, jailed, and chained to a prison wall for doing just that. Upon their release, they headed to Thessalonica to do it all again. They arrived at the local synagogue to give evidence that *"This Jesus...is the Christ"* (Acts 17:3). Some believed. Some disbelieved and wrote off the church as being out of step with the modern world. And then there were some who hung around to *"stir up the crowd"* (v. 8), much like those inciting current-day protestors to riot.

The pair were seen as *"men who have upset the world"* (v. 6) or *"these are the men who have who turned the world upside down and have now come here"* (PHILLIPS). Paul and Silas built for themselves quite a name in the region. The ancient world saw (and the world today still does, by the way) Christians as men and women fashioned after the likes of Elijah, whose reputation was that of a *"troubler of Israel"* (I Kings 18:17). I'm thinking that early church members probably wore team jerseys with the title *"Troublemakers"* (agitators, disruptors of the peace) printed across their chest.

Proclaim *"another king"* (Acts 17:7) other than *"Caesar"* and watch what happens. Confront a "stubborn and obstinate" people who live out their daily lives as they please, as if there is no God, and rocks will be thrown, the streets will burn, and fists will fly. Go ahead and point out lifestyles that embrace idolatry in its many forms, promote immorality as the "new normal," accept adultery as justifiable behavior, encourage financial greed and "dishonest gain" as a way to get ahead in life, or dare to call abortion what it is—murder and the sacrifice of our children to the god of convenience—(just to name a few issues—cf. Ezek. 22:1-12) and watch the trouble begin. If you insist that the culture change its attitude, replace its values, and adopt another worldview other than the one accepted by the general population, converting to one that promotes a biblical approach to life, you had better be prepared to duck. Encourage others to live as God wants, in compliance with His revealed Word—a rather unpopular message, and look out. Men love *"darkness rather than the Light; for their deeds were evil"* (John 3:19), and they will buck up in defiance every time when pressed to give account and/or take responsibility for behavior outside the boundaries of moral decency and God's ideals. The Burger King slogan "Have it your way!" rules modern-day life. Ignoring biblical principles and turning life upside down from the way God intended is a common approach to daily living in today's world. *"Everyone did what was right in his own eyes"* (Judges 21:25) has proven to be a perennial problem for the human race throughout the ages.

The description of these early Christians as those *"who have upset the world"* caught my attention and forced me to think about the influence of my own life and the impact it may or may not have had in my generation and potentially on into the next. A little self-reflection can be painfully revealing. Regardless, I thought it best to examine the character of my own faith, the strength of my personal convictions, the power of my words to influence, and the force of my actions to bring about positive change in my little corner of my world. I wonder…*have I been effective in my daily walk with Christ to disrupt the thinking, values, and standards of a world system turned upside down? Have I the spiritual fortitude and guts to attempt to turn that world right side up with the message of the gospel, made evident in and through the manner in which I have lived my life day to day?* These are hard questions, which serve to reinforce my suspicions. I have a good deal of personal work to do in this regard, and I must do better and live deeper in a shallow, self-centered world, especially if I want my life to count for something positive.

Philip Eaton wrote, "We must affirm the story of what is true and good and beautiful, our ancient Christian story, right in the midst of a culture that has grown profoundly suspicious of calling anything true."[3] Deep people are busy seeking opportunities to engage the culture and change the world in meaningful ways. They are pro-active because they are pro-Christ, and thus willing to "commit to being in the mix,"[4] ready to jump into the thick of things. Mark Galli, in writing for *Christianity Today*, said that "Christians ought to be people who practice making life beautiful"[5]—not just different but more appealing, more kind, more efficient, more productive, more purposeful—simply better than it has ever been before. That must be the reputation and function of those living deep in a shallow world.

The call to follow Jesus into the *"the highways and back alleys"* (Luke 14:23, CEB) remains the same even to this day. *"I will make you fishers of men"* was the call of Christ to His disciples to turn the world right side up. That deal is still on the table—an opportunity to make life something special—"catching" the hearts and minds of men and women everywhere, right where we live, *"even to the remotest part of the earth"* (Acts 1:8). It was (and is) a divine summons to live deeply.

The disciples did what men should do when God signals for them to follow. They immediately dropped their nets, left behind everything they knew, got "in the mix," and set out to capture the souls of men. Success demands deep commitment. Little did those disciples know that their actions would soon impact the world for the better and change the course of eternity for so many. No longer would they be gutting fish for a living. Instead, their task would be to bring the truth and the transforming power of the gospel to improve the lives of their generation and beyond, touching the physical, social, moral, and most importantly the spiritual needs of people.

If there was ever a time for the church to engage the current culture and move the world toward a better place, it's now. This modern age and present generation is beset with confusion and muddled thinking. No longer is the world sure about much of anything—identity, human dignity, sexuality and intimacy, relationships, marriage, divorce and remarriage, family dynamics, mental and emotional health issues, faith, hope, love, and all the rest. Currently the world is lost in a maze of pluralism and moral independence. The potential for followers of Christ to affect change in the world (and that includes in the home, church, and community) and influence the next generation for the good has always been present, maybe more so today than ever before. We need deep people who reflect the passion of Christ to recognize and seize the opportunities set before them to define godly values, encourage biblical behavior, and change a toxic culture that is ever changing and self-destructing.

January 1, 404 AD, Telemachus went to a gladiatorial match in Rome; Christians usually avoided these events. When this man attended, his conscience gave him no rest as he watched two heavily armed men attempt to kill each other for the entertainment of the crowd. The sight of such brutality pressed Telemachus into daring action. No longer could he remain silent or still. He became personally involved, jumping down onto the arena floor and running to separate the pair of gladiators who were locked in mortal combat. He screamed, "Don't do this. Don't kill each other…This is murder." The crowd was so incensed by his interruption that they stoned him to death. He died in the Colosseum, trying to change a violent society with little regard for the value of human life (an all-too-familiar scene) and bent on destroying itself. As a result of his courage and selfless action, all future gladiatorial contests were banned by the emperor, and countless lives were saved.[6] Deep people live and die to change their world for the better.

The pages of church history are written by the gallant acts of men and women who have upset the world and turned it right side up. Martin Luther, the Reformation leader who insisted on biblical truth as the uncompromising standard by which to guide daily living and church doctrine, challenged the religious "good ol' boys" of the Vatican, the money grabbing clergy of the church in their selling of indulgences, and a power-hungry Pope demanding allegiance and loyalty to his rule. Then Luther did the unthinkable, translating the Bible into the common language of the day and opening the Scriptures to the minds and hearts of millions. He angered those in power; they burned his books in Rome's Piazza Navona and hauled him before a religious court to face charges of heresy. Pope Leo X described Luther as a "wild boar from the forest."[7] But no matter, Luther turned his world right side up—a deep man, doing deep things, to produce deep results.

Fabiola, a wealthy Roman noblewoman, converted to Christianity and then devoted herself to care for the poor and the sick. She founded the first civilian public hospital in western Europe (AD 394). Thousands attended her funeral, where she was remembered by St. Jerome for her unselfishness and devotion to the least fortunate members of society.[8] She made a difference, something people with deep convictions and a deeper commitment to Christ look to do regularly. She turned her world right side up.

Catherine of Siena died in Rome at the age of 33 in 1380. She lived a life of service and compassion, lovingly caring for those in great need. When the plague struck her hometown in 1374, most people fled, but she stuck around to minister to the hopelessly ill and to bury the dead, a job nobody else wanted. She turned her world right side up.[9]

William Wilberforce, a member of the English Parliament, a social reformer, and a strong Christian, spent the better part of his public life as a leader of the abolition movement to end England's involvement with the Transatlantic Slave Trade. For eighteen years he regularly introduced anti-slavery motions in parliament until it was passed in 1833. He too turned his world right side up.[10]

Oswald Chambers was a humble man who once wrote, "It takes

me a long while to realize that God has no respect for anything I bring him. All he wants from me is unconditional surrender." And surrender he did, having been converted under the ministry of Charles Spurgeon. Chambers became a teacher through the League of Prayer, he opened the Bible Training College to better equip men wanting to serve the local church, and he ministered as an itinerant preacher proclaiming the good news of the gospel. He also entered the military during WW I as a chaplain, sharing Christ with soldiers amid the chaos of blood and tears—a distinguished career serving the kingdom of God. After just fifteen years in public ministry, Chambers died suddenly of appendicitis. Later his wife published his devotional *My Utmost for His Highest*, which turned his world and the generations to come right side up.[11] His life and ministry made a difference to so many, and his influence continues to this day.

Billy Graham, one of the world's foremost evangelists, preached to thousands in a ministry that spanned decades. In the 1973 crusade in South Korea, 1.1 million people showed up for that single event. The picture of the crowd in attendance is overwhelming. It stands as testimony to Graham's deep love and concern for the souls of people. He was also a friend to presidents and kings from across the globe. He traveled the world and across the United States. But everywhere he went, he integrated his crusades and revival meetings when it was unfashionable to do so, breaking down the racial barriers that had separated one man from another. The gospel, he believed, was for all men, regardless of the color of their skin, their ethnic background, or their social standing.[12] He turned the world right side up.

Joseph de Veuster (Father Damien) joined the Society of the Sacred Hearts of Jesus and Mary at Leuven, Belgium, and was ordained a Catholic priest in 1864. He set up his mission in Kalaupapa, a community of lepers on the island of Molokai in Hawaii. People who suffered from the dreaded disease were banished to the colony—isolated, forgotten, and left to die in deplorable and desperate conditions. For sixteen years, Father Damien lived among the people and served them as both pastor and physician with little assistance from the church or the island government. He willingly lived among the helpless and the hopeless, treating each one with dignity, compassion, and a deep sense of care for their physical and spiritual well-being.

Father Damien also developed housing, improved the colony's water and food supply, built two orphanages and a church, and bandaged the wounds of the people. In 1884, he contracted leprosy but would not leave the island for treatment. He stayed at his post until he breathed his last and was buried on the island as he requested. His body was later exhumed and returned to Belgium, but the people of Kalaupapa did not forget his kindness or his ministry. They petitioned the Belgium authorities, requesting that they send back his right hand to be buried in the original grave on Molokai—the very hand that had touched with the love of Christ those nobody else would touch, the hand that turned the world right side up.[13]

Frankly, I feel dwarfed in the presence of such deep men and women who served Christ, His church, and the world so well. But such ministry doesn't come without a price. No service of this depth and for the kingdom of God comes cheaply. Should you *"upset the world,"* you will most likely pay dearly and personally for your efforts. Holy action is always disturbing and downright dangerous to the status quo both inside and outside the church.

For instance, when Jeremiah challenged the current issues of his day, he was thrown into a mud pit to shut him up. Daniel refused to go along with the crowd and opted rather to follow his religious convictions, which resulted in his being served up as lunch for the lions. Paul challenged the lucrative practice of fortunetelling in the city of Thyatira, which got him beaten and sent on a quick trip to the local jail.

On another occasion, while waiting in Athens for the arrival of Silas and Timothy, Paul was *"troubled"* deeply (Acts 17:16, TPT) by what he saw. The city had become a *"junkyard of idols"* (MSG). I suspect the apostle understood the destructive nature of idolatry. He had, of course, the equivalent of a Ph.D. in religion and was certainly aware of the Old Testament *"examples"* of those who were *"destroyed by the destroyer"* for their idol worship and the accompanying immorality, pagan practices, and temple sacrifices (cf. I Cor. 10:5-14). He wrote the Corinthians (an imperative here) to *"flee from idolatry"* (II Corinthians 10:14) for it leads men away from the truth and destroys their ability to make sound judgments and good decisions. Idols, in whatever form they come, are a poor substitute for the real thing. So Paul spoke up and faithfully delivered the *"word of God"* (v. 13) to a people needing a better way to live—the only way, the only life, and the only truth.

John Wesley wrote,

> Condemn no man for not thinking as you think. Let everyone enjoy the full and free liberty of thinking for himself. Let every man use his own judgment, since every man must give an account of himself to God…if you cannot reason nor persuade a man into the truth, never attempt to force a man into it. If love will not compel him to come, leave him to God, the judge of all.[14]

A good piece of advice for men and women living deep in a fallen world.

In the closing scene of *The Lord of the Rings*, the young hobbit, Frodo, lamented over all the tragedy and darkness that had befallen him. He had seen much in his journey—destruction, disaster, death—more than any individual should have to witness and experience. He moaned, "I wish it need not have happened in my time."[15]

Frankly, me too! I wish life were easier. I do like comfort, tranquility, stability, and the like. Instead, what I've seen and experienced (like many of you) has been the disruption of my daily plans, a broken heart, lost dreams, unfilled goals, unexpected painful tragedy, and moral weakness. The heartache runs deep. And like Frodo, "I wish it need not have happened in my time." I wish I did not have to see a world (or my own life) turned upside down.

Gandalf the Grey, Frodo's ever wise mentor, consoled the anxious hobbit with these words:

> So do all who live to see such times, but that is not for them to decide. All we have to decide is what to do with the time that is given to us. There are other forces at work in this world, Frodo, besides the will of evil.[16]

That is an encouraging thought—*"other forces at work."* It suggests that evil is not running unhindered or unchecked. From a biblical perspective, the *"forces,"* (no reference to *Star Wars*' "May the force be with you") include the power of the goodness and faithfulness of God to restrict and restrain hell's objectives. When my day has been turned upside down (and it happens frequently) and evil seems to be winning out, I've got to remember that God is *"at work in this world"* and in my life to turn it right side up, regardless of appearances or how I may feel at the moment. I want to play a part in that divine plan.

Subsequently, I must decide *"what to do with the time given me."* Now I have a choice. I can go one way or the other. I can run scared. I can cower in fear. I can permit disappointment, hatred, bitterness, and anger to overwhelm my thoughts and ravage my spirit. If I so choose, I can live in despondency, crippled by discouragement and disillusionment. These are options…not good ones, but options, nonetheless.

There is a better choice about *"what to do with the time given me"*: turn the world right side up. I can get up, stand up, move up to make life better…no longer a victim of evil, but a force to be reckoned with, a person uniquely designed and sacredly equipped to be used of God to carry out heaven's plan in my little corner of the world, no matter what I must face. That's what deep people do.

Make no mistake. The Christian is ordered to the "front lines" by divine decree. The battle plans from eternity past have been drawn; I have my place in the fight, and so do you. Jesus prayed, *"Father, I do not ask You to take them out of the world, but to keep them from evil… As You did send Me into the world, I also have sent them into the world"* (John 17:15-18).

Living deep in a shallow world means I am spending *"the time given me"* choosing to live in the light of the sovereignty, wisdom, and Word of God, rather than running off with my tail between my legs, wallowing in debilitating self-pity and leaving the world around me a mess, without direction and with no frame of reference. Better to *"fight the good fight of faith"* (I Tim. 6:12) to turn the world right side up and deny evil its say.

Several years ago *USA Today* reported on an 86-year-old woman, Joy Johnson, who had run in 25 New York City marathons. She ran her first race at 61 years of age. In her last event, she had fallen along the way but got up and eventually completed the course and crossed the finish line in about eight hours. She was a devout Christian, often singing hymns as she ran. On her kitchen wall was hung the words of Isaiah 41:31—*"Those who wait for the Lord…will run and not get tired."*

Shortly after the race, she returned to her motel room, laid down, fell asleep, and never woke up. The article noted that she had "died with her running shoes on."[17] Those words caught my attention. That's how I want to live. That's how I want to die—in my "running shoes," serving God, fulfilling His call upon my life, living deep, turning the world right side up, and finishing the race strong.

Endnotes

[1] Maisie Ward, *Gilbert Keith Chesterton* (Oxford: Rowman & Littlefield Publishers, Inc, 2006), 398.

[2] Alan Noble, *Disruptive Witness: Speaking Truth in a Distracted Age* (Downers Grove, Ill.: IVP Books, 2018), 30.

[3] Philip W. Eaton, *Engaging the Culture, Changing the Word* (Downers Grove, Ill.: InterVarsity, 2011), 8.

[4] Eaton, *Engaging the Culture, Changing the Word*, 28.

[5] Mark Galli, "Beautiful Orthodoxy," *Christianity Today*, Oct. 2016, 38.

[6] Glenn Sunshine, "6 Christians Who Changed the World," *Summit Ministries*, Oct 14, 2015, retrieved from https://www.summit.org/resources/articles/6-christians-who-changed-the-world/.

[7] Douglas O. Linder, "The Trial of Martin Luther: An Account," *Famous Trials, 1995-2020*, retrieved from https://famous-trials.com/luther/286-home.

[8] Diane K. Hawkins, "Fabiola," Apr. 20, 2020, *Encyclopedia.com*,

https://www.encyclopedia.com/science/encyclopedias-almanacs-transcripts-and-maps/fabiola.

[9]"Catherine of Siena—Mystic and Political Activist," *Christianity Today*, Aug. 8, 2008.

[10]Oswald Chambers, "Preacher Who Gave His Utmost," *Christianity Today*, retrieved from https://www.christianitytoday.com/history/people/innertravelers/oswald-chambers.html.

[11]History, "William Wilberforce" (1759-1833), *BBC*, http://www.bbc.co.uk/history/historic_figures/wilberforce_william.shtml.

[12]Jeffrey L. Sheler, *Billy Graham: America's Preacher 1918-2118* (New York: Time Books, 2018), 73.

[13]The Editors of Encyclopaedia Britannica, "St. Damien of Molokai, Belgian Priest," *Encyclopedia Britannica*, retrieved from https://www.britannica.com/biography/Saint-Damien-of-Molokai.

[14]John Wesley, "The Works of the Rev. John Wesley: The eighteenth, nineteenth, twentieth, and twenty-first numbers of his journal, particular of his death, review of his character, etc.," retrieved from https://www.azquotes.com/quote/1311374.421.

[15]J. R. R. Tolkien (novel), Fran Walsh (screenplay), *The Lord of the Rings: The Fellowship of the Rings*, New Line Cinema, 2001.

[16]Tolkien, *The Lord of the Rings: The Fellowship of the Rings*.

[17]Michael Winter, "NYC Marathoner, 86, Dies after Her 25th Race," *USA TODAY* (11-5-13).

I Dreamed of Heaven
I dreamed death came the other night:
And heaven's gates swung wide.
With kindly grace an angel
Ushered me inside.
And there, to my astonishment,
Stood folks I'd known on earth.
Some I'd judged and labeled
Unfit or of little worth.
Indignant words rose to my lips,
But never were set free;
For every face showed stunned surprise…
No one expected me!
– C. R. Hembree

Chapter 12

Sounding the Alarm

In the Revelation of Jesus Christ, John recorded a sobering vision.

"And then I saw a great white throne, and one seated upon it from whose presence both earth and sky fled and vanished. Then I saw the dead, great and small, standing before the throne and *the books were opened. And another book was opened, which is the book of life. And the dead were judged by what was written in the books concerning what they had done"* (Revelation 20:11-12, PHILLIPS).

The description of that great event at the close of the ages brings me up short, to say the least. It's breathtaking. It's sobering and difficult to grasp the magnitude and scope of what is to come. For a moment, picture every man or woman who has ever lived (including "yours truly"), standing nervously before the tribunal of God, awaiting their trial to commence in God's courtroom before the entire universe.

The thought is rather unnerving and intimidating. It should be. I am going to be found out. I am guilty, and I might add embarrassed, at being a transgressor of God's laws. There is no denying it. The facts and "nothing but the facts" (for you *Dragnet* fans) speak for themselves. The entire scene is alarming! A day of accountability is coming when the scales of justice will be balanced. You can count on it and best not take it lightly. *"Do not be deceived,"* wrote Paul to the Galatians, "God is not mocked [He will not allow Himself to be ridiculed, nor treated with contempt nor allow His precepts to be scornfully set aside]; for whatever a man sows, this and this only is what he will reap" (Gal. 6:7, AMP). Rather sobering.

One day I was driving home from a school event, listening to Christian radio. The program was definitely geared for the younger set. The DJ was praying for a young man who had called into the show about some problem he was experiencing. The host began his prayer with these words, *"O God, You are so cool!"* In all fairness, I think he was trying to connect with the teen, but his words came across as rather shallow. They just rubbed me the wrong way. I'm not sure if I would have referred to the God Who sits on the great white throne as "so cool." He is much bigger, more fearsome, and more dangerous than anything our imaginations could possibly conjure up.

A. W. Tozer commented,

> It is my opinion that the Christian conception of God current in the middle years of the 20th century (and this extends to our current generation and culture) is so decadent as to be utterly beneath the dignity of the Most High God and actually constitutes for professed believers something amounting to a moral calamity.[1]

One author defined God as "The old guy. Long white beard. Voice like thunder. Fingertips that flash lightning. Gets really ticked when I fashion calves out of gold." Talk about shallow thinking! I asked my students one day to write down a description of God, Who He is and what He is like? Here are several of their responses.

- "I don't know Him well enough to tell you." *(Fair enough and honest)*

- "I really don't know; maybe I'll find out in due time." *(I certainly hope so.)*

- "God is our Father in heaven, infinite, but I can't wrap my head around Him." *(Not to worry, nobody else can either.)*

- "There is no God, but the gods that most people believe in originated with the creation myths of Genesis." *(A fantasy? Really? Only a fool would say that—Psalm 14:1.)*

Yuri Gagarin, the Russian cosmonaut, had the privilege of piloting man's first flight into space. Nikita Khrushchev (you know, the guy who pounded his shoe on a desk at the United Nations) said mockingly of Gagarin's accomplishment, "Why didn't you step on the brakes in front of God? Here is Gagarin, who flew up to space, and yet, even he didn't see God anywhere."[2] Russia's idea of anti-religious propaganda at its finest.

W. A. Criswell of First Baptist Church, Dallas, responded, "If he had stepped out of his spacesuit, he would have seen God."[3] Yuri Gagarin died in 1968. He no longer has any doubts about the existence and justice of God. Nor does Khrushchev. And neither do deep people living in a shallow world.

Deep people know God, or at the very least, they want to know God, the God of the Scriptures, the God Who is clothed in the royal robes of glory and divine splendor, the God of immeasurable power, righteousness, and wisdom beyond human imagination, a holy God Who promises to one day *"punish the world for its evil and the wicked for their iniquity"* (Isa. 13:11). But this same God is also presented in the Bible as a father to the fatherless, a husband to the widow, the lifter of my head, the lover of my soul, my protector, my provider, my redeemer, my all in all, the healer of my diseases, the God Who *"satisfies your [and my] years with good things."* He is *"compassionate and gracious, slow to anger and abounding in lovingkindness… [and] mindful that we are but dust"* (cf. Psalm 103:1-14). He is all of that and so much more. He is *"the Alpha and the Omega…who is and who was and who is to come, the Almighty"* (Rev. 1:8), and He is to be feared, revered, and loved *"because He first loved us"* (I John 4:19). A deep man knows God, as well as any man can, and has caught a glimpse of His power and lordship, yet is comforted by knowing the matchless love of God the Father. He lives each day as a testimony to the greatest truth of all—*"Jesus loves me, this I know, for the Bible tells me so."*

Sounding the Alarm

The Bible teaches three primary truths about the God of the Bible (cf. Isa. 43:11-13, 44:6-8, Gen. 1:1, Deut. 6:4, Psa. 90:2, Rom. 1:20). These truths are foundational to deep living.

1) *There is a God.* Nowhere does the Bible set out to prove the existence of God. Rather, it assumes the existence of God from cover to cover and does so with a vengeance.

2) *There is no god but this God.* Search high and low throughout the known universe and beyond. Build all the golden calves you want. Beat yourself silly on Mt. Carmel with the prophets of Baal, screaming for their gods (any god for that matter) to answer, to do something, anything. But nothing of any consequence will happen. Nada. Zero. Nobody is listening, none are able to respond. Powerless. Helpless—gods made in the image of man. In the end, you will discover that there is but one true God Who exists. The Apostle Paul wrote to young Timothy, *"There is one God and one Mediator who can reconcile God and humanity—the man Christ Jesus"* (I Tim. 2:5, NLT). He alone will answer your call and satisfy your deepest needs.

3) *There is no god like this God.* It is impossible to put God in a box and figure Him out. Try as you will (as I have), it's not ever going to happen. He is utterly unique, and as the theologians (Kierkegaard, Sproul, etc.) like to say, God is "wholly other." That's about the best some of the smartest minds in the world could come up with. He's just different, unlike anything or anyone we've ever known within the sphere of our experience. There is no one (outside of Jesus, His only begotten Son) to whom we might compare God and nothing from which we might gain little more than a superficial understanding of the

full majesty and substance of His nature. Unless He chooses to reveal Himself (and He did in Christ), He remains hidden, incomprehensible and a constant mystery—a stranger, if you will—for *"No man hath seen God at any time"* (John 1:18, KJV).

Everything we know of God from the Scriptures can fit into one of these three categories, including His wrath and the coming great white throne judgment, as well as His grace and mercy in Christ Jesus. Both the justice of God and the love of God come together simultaneously at the cross of Christ. That is the straightforward message (metanarrative) of the Bible from Genesis to Revelation—creation, the fall, redemption. Any man or woman whose sins are forgiven by almighty God and who commits his/her life and future to Jesus, trusting the destiny of his/her soul to the person and work of Christ (the starting point for living a deeper life), becomes a grateful recipient of God's amazing grace and divine love and the beneficiary of an incredible gift—the joy of eternity, life unending in the presence of the Savior and the saints, and a few mansions thrown into the deal! That is good news for all mankind. But the story doesn't end there.

The prophets of old and the writers of the New Testament warned of an impending disaster of cosmic proportions and certain judgment—*"the coming of the great and dreadful day of the LORD"* (Joel 2:31, NIV). The prophetic word pulls no punches, sounding the alarm loud and clear: apart from Christ, all men remain lost and die in their sins. The consequences of man's rejection of God's gracious offer to rescue and save are catastrophic and eternal.

Genuine believers recognize the reality of the risks ahead and look for occasions to issue a warning to an unsuspecting world and to do so with a profound sense of urgency, being deeply concerned for the future well-being of every individual. The threat of eternal calamity hangs over the head of all humanity like Damocles' sword—an imminent and ever-present danger. This is real. This is not "fake news." The world needs a *"watchman"* (a deep man or woman) who sees *"the sword coming"* and will *"blow the trumpet"* of warning, the gospel of Jesus Christ found in the Word of God (cf. Ezek. 33:6-7). The task of those living deep is not simply to announce the terrifying wrath of God (that's just part of the redemptive story) but to deliver the hope of the good news of God's incredible love. My responsibility in following hard after Christ is to point my neighbors, friends, and family toward the cross and the grace and mercy of God as the only way out of the mess the world is in. Vance Havner was correct. "The tragedy of our time is that the situation is desperate but the saints are not."[4]

Early Sunday morning, April 15, 2012, at 12:15 a.m., a tornado hit the quiet community of Woodward, Oklahoma. The storm struck with merciless, unforeseen power—high winds and baseball-size hail, destroying and damaging houses, a hospital, a jail, and parts of an Air Force base along the way. Few knew it was coming. Most were sleeping—unsuspecting, unwary, and unaware of the imminent danger. Tragically, eighty-three homes were destroyed, and five people needlessly died.

Mayor Roscoe Hill explained, "The sirens were apparently not working when the tornado struck."[5] No forewarning was issued. No alert was given. No alarm was sounded, just a peculiar, eerie silence in the face of peril that left many unprepared…and some dead.

Yvonne Tucker, a survivor of the storm, looked at the damage around her neighborhood and community. She voiced, "I didn't know what to do or where to go…It is unreal. I just feel lost."[6]

How sobering—the thought of lives lost because the sirens failed.

I am reminded that life, death, and eternity all hinge on the "sirens" working, doing what they were designed to do, expected to do, must do. I stand convicted by my own words. I must do better.

My life and ministry must compassionately and clearly sound the alarm of the coming "storm of judgment"—that awful day when every man and woman, *"both great and small,"* will appear before the tribunal of God to give account for his/her actions. The Book of Life and the Book of Deeds will be open, and there will be "no place to hide," nowhere to run (Rev. 20:11-12, NLT). No storm shelters. No excuses. No explanations will be necessary or tolerated. No weak or flimsy justification for questionable character and poor conduct will be allowed. No attempt to explain away or excuse destructive behavior, unkind actions, self-serving attitudes, and biting words will be acceptable. Failure to bind up the wounds of the broken-hearted, to give drink to the thirsty, or to offer clothes to the naked—every action and motive will be revealed. Each man and woman will be held personally and morally responsible for the life he or she has chosen to live. Let me sound the warning "siren" loud and strong: *"The wages of sin is death, but the free gift of God is eternal life through Christ Jesus our Lord"* (Rom. 6:23, NLT).

The clear, distinct message of the gospel is a summons to safety for all men and women everywhere to run to the only place of refuge and shelter—the foot of the cross—and to do so before the thunder and lightning of judgment strikes. *"Truly, truly, I say to you, whoever hears my word and believes him who sent me has eternal life. He does not come into judgment, but has passed from death to life"* (John 5:24, ESV). When the opportunity presents itself, people who live deep stand ready to issue the alarm. They know the truth—to reject or ignore Christ Jesus, Who came to love and rescue the world not to condemn it or *"judge"* it (cf. John 3:17) but to redeem sinners and reconcile God and man, is to forfeit eternal life. *"For unless you believe that I AM who I claim to be* [God come in the flesh, the great I AM clothed with power and all authority, the risen Lord of the ages, the Creator of the ends of the earth and beyond, the lover and redeemer of your soul, the Christ–the Son of the living God], *you will die in your sins"* (John 8:24, NLT).

Here are the only two options: I will either stand before God on my own merits (and there aren't many), cowering in fear while the *"accuser"* (Rev. 12:10) reads the charges leveled against me and points his ugly finger in my direction, or I will stand before God the Judge of judges with the greatest defense attorney the world has ever seen at my side, Jesus, Who alone is willing and able to successfully take up my cause. Take your pick. One or the other.

> *But if anyone does sin [and that's going to happen], we have an advocate who pleads our case before the Father. He is Jesus Christ, the one who is truly righteous. He himself is the sacrifice that atones for our sins—and not only our sins but the sins of all the world* (I John 2:1-2).

Let's face it. Apart from Christ, I have no hope of acquittal. Nor do I have a legal right to expect mercy for my criminal activity, the multiple daily offenses committed against God and people over the course of my life. They are all listed on my miserable record. That's the raw reality of my predicament. But redemption is just as real, maybe more so. A Savior has atoned for my cosmic treason, making known the mercy and love of God at Calvary and offering redemption to all who would take hold of it. *"The gospel,"* wrote Paul, *"is the power of God for salvation to everyone who believes"* (Rom. 1:16, ESV). The divine message is the "old rugged cross," or it's nothing at all.

Sin and despair, like the sea waves cold,
Threaten the soul with infinite loss;
Grace that is greater, yes, grace untold,
Points to the refuge, the mighty cross.

Grace, grace, God's grace,
Grace that will pardon and cleanse within;
Grace, grace, God's grace,
Grace that is greater than all our sin![7]

Deep living demands we share such good news of the gospel—more real, more true, more powerful *"than all our sin."*

I wouldn't be here if it weren't for my aunt's faithfulness and love for God and for her family. She sounded the alarm on May 15, 1957. I attended a Billy Graham Crusade at Madison Square Garden in New York City with my mother at the invitation of my loving aunt. The Word was proclaimed that evening with clarity and power. I remember it well, like it was yesterday. The "alert" went out, the gospel was presented, an invitation was given, and an 11-year-old boy, who didn't understand much about all it meant, was captivated and captured by the love of God in Christ, stepped out of his seat, and walked unaccompanied down to the arena floor. *"Just as I am, without one plea, But that Thy blood was shed for me."* Some years later God called that same boy to seminary, to the pastorate, and eventually to the halls of a Christian college because somebody loved him enough to sound the alarm. The warning saved my life and my soul.

I may not ever be a rich man, but I have enjoyed a richness and depth to life that no amount of money could ever buy. I have often told my friends, "If you leave your children all the wealth this world has to offer but have not left them Jesus, you left them nothing of lasting

Sounding the Alarm

value or substance; but if you have left them Jesus and left them nothing of this world, you have left them everything they need for this life and the life to come."

My aunt left me Jesus...and with Him, eternity thrown into the mix, as well as the privilege of serving the kingdom of God for many years and the honor of preaching the funeral service to celebrate her life.

As I consider her life, two simple words defined her—*"Jesus Saves!"* Nothing else really mattered to her but *"Jesus Saves."* She spoke that message. She lived that message. She went out into eternity and passed through the gates of Heaven, rejoicing with that message on her lips. To anyone who would listen, she testified of the love of God and the sacrifice of Christ on the cross, where redeeming blood was shed to secure salvation for all people from every nation and tribe. She sounded the alarm boldly, without apology, but always with a sense of compassion, concern, and deep love for people and the eternal state of their souls.

I am reminded of a 15-year-old girl who years ago handed me a section (stanza 2) of the poem, *What Then*, written by J. Whitfield Green. I've kept it with me for nearly 50 years.

> When the choir has sung its last anthem,
> And the preacher has made his last prayer;
> When the people have heard their last sermon,
> And the sound has died out in the air;
> When the Bible lies closed on the altar,
> And the pews all empty of men;
> And each one stands facing his record,
> And the Great Book is opened—WHAT THEN?

Indeed...what then? Sound the alarm. It's what deep people do.

Endnotes

[1] A. W. Tozer, *The Knowledge of the Holy* (New York: Harper Collins, 1961), 3.

[2] Columnists, "Yuri Gagarin, First Human in Space, Was a Devout Christian, Says His Close Friend," Belief Net/On the Front Lines of the Culture Wars, April 2011, retrieved from https://www.beliefnet.com/columnists/on_the_front_lines_of_the_culture_wars/2011/04/yuri-gagarin-first-human-in-space-was-a-devout-christian-says-his-close-friend.html.

[3] Charles Swindoll, "Charles Swindoll: Illustrating So People Will Listen," *Church Leaders*, June 13:2012, 4-5, Retrieved from https://churchleaders.com/pastors/pastor-articles/161311-charles-swindoll-illustrating-so-people-will-listen.html/5.

[4] David R. Smith, "Vance Havner on Christian Devotion," *It's Like This*, Nov 3, 2011, retrieved from http://www.itslikethis.org/vance-havner-on-christian-devotion/.

[5] Associated Press, "At Least 5 Dead after Severe Weather Hits the Plains," *CBS News*, April 15, 2012, retrieved from https://www.cbsnews.com/news/at-least-5-dead-after-severe-weather-hits-the-plains/.

[6] "At Least 5 Dead after Severe Weather Hits the Plains," *CBS News*, April 15, 2012,

[7] Julia H. Johnston, "Grace Greater Than All My Sin," Ed. Wesley L. Forbis, *The Baptist Hymnal* (Nashville: Convention Press, 1991), 329.

Epilogue

Avery T. Willis (1934-2010) served the church as a missionary, Christian educator, author (Master Life Series), and senior vice president for the SBC Mission Board. The following words were attributed to Willis but reportedly written originally by an African pastor who had tacked them on the wall of his house. I am not sure whether the quote originated with Willis or the African pastor. But it doesn't matter. The powerful statement stands on its own merit, applicable to every Christ follower. It serves as a description of what a man (or woman) with deep convictions, living in a shallow world, truly looks and sounds like.

Lord, disturb me as I consider the depth of my own Christian life. May I grow to be known as a deep man of faith who loves God and loves people.

My Commitment as a Christian

I'm a part of the fellowship of the unashamed. I have Holy Spirit power. The die has been cast. I have stepped over the line. The decision has been made. I'm a disciple of His. I won't look back, let up, slow down, back away, or be still.

My past is redeemed, my present makes sense, my future is secure. I'm finished and done with low living, sight walking, small planning, smooth knees, colorless dreams, tamed visions, mundane talking, cheap living, and dwarfed goals.

I no longer need pre-eminence, prosperity, position, promotions, plaudits, or popularity. I don't have to be right, first, tops, recognized, praised, regarded or rewarded. I live by faith, lean on His presence, walk by patience, lift by prayer, and labor by power.

My face is set, my gait is fast, my goal is heaven, my road is narrow, my way rough, my companions few, my Guide reliable, my mission clear. I cannot be bought, compromised, detoured, lured away, turned back, deluded or delayed. I will not flinch in the face of sacrifice, hesitate in the presence of the adversary, negotiate at the table of the enemy, ponder at the pool of popularity, or meander in the maze of mediocrity.

I won't give up, shut up, let up, until I have stayed up, stored up, prayed up, paid up, preached up for the cause of Christ.

I am a disciple of Jesus. I must go till He comes, give till I drop, preach till all know, and work till He stops me. And when He does come for His own, He will have no problems recognizing me—my banner will be clear!

Lord, I need to go deeper...

Bibliography

Unless otherwise noted Scripture quotations are taken from the New American Standard Bible® (NASB), Copyright © 1960, 1962, 1963, 1968, 1971, 1972, 1973,1975, 1977, 1995 by The Lockman Foundation. Used by permission. www.Lockman.org.

Scripture quotations marked (AMP) are taken from the Amplified® Bible, Copyright © 2015 by The Lockman Foundation. Used by permission. www.Lockman.org.

The Holy Bible, Berean Study Bible, (BSB), Copyright ©2016, 2018 by Bible Hub. Used by Permission. All Rights Reserved Worldwide.

Scriptures marked (CEB) are taken from The Common English Bible (CEB) Website, https://www.commonenglishbible.com/ and used within stated restrictions.

Scripture quotations marked (ESV) are from The Holy Bible, English Standard Version® (ESV®), copyright © 2001 by Crossway, a publishing ministry of Good News Publishers. Used by permission. All rights reserved."

Scriptures marked (KJV) are taken from the KING JAMES VERSION (KJV): KING JAMES VERSION, public domain.

Scripture quotations marked (MSG) are taken from THE MESSAGE, copyright © 1993, 1994, 1995, 1996, 2000, 2001, 2002 by Eugene H. Peterson. Used by permission of NavPress. All rights reserved. Represented by Tyndale House Publishers, Inc.

Scripture marked (NKJV) taken from the New King James Version®. Copyright © 1982 by Thomas Nelson. Used by permission. All rights reserved.

Scripture quotations marked (NRSV) are from the New Revised Standard Version Bible, copyright © 1989 the Division of Christian Education of the National Council of the Churches of Christ in the United States of America. Used by permission. All rights reserved.

Scripture quotations marked (NIV) are taken from the Holy Bible, New International Version®, NIV®. Copyright © 1973, 1978, 1984, 2011 by Biblica, Inc.™ Used by permission of Zondervan. All rights reserved worldwide. www.zondervan.com The "NIV" and "New International Version" are trademarks registered in the United States Patent and Trademark Office by Biblica, Inc.™

Scripture quotations marked (NLT) are taken from the Holy Bible, New Living Translation copyright © 1996, 2004, 2007 by Tyndale House Foundation. Used by permission of Tyndale House Publishers Inc., Carol Stream, IL 60188. All rights reserved. New Living, NLT, and the New Living Translation logo are registered trademarks of Tyndale House Publishers.

Scripture quotations marked (Phillips) are taken from The New Testament in Modern English, copyright 1958, 1959, 1960 J.B. Phillips and 1947, 1952, 1955, 1957, 1976 The MacMillan Company, New York. Used by permission. All rights reserved.

Scripture quotations marked (TPT) are from The Passion Translation®. Copyright © 2017, 2018 by Passion & Fire Ministries, Inc. Used by permission. All rights reserved. ThePassionTranslation.com.

www.ingramcontent.com/pod-product-compliance
Lightning Source LLC
Chambersburg PA
CBHW072137160426
43197CB00012B/2143